P9-DNB-535

SMALL CRAFT
MAINTENANCE

SMALL CRAFT MAINTENANCE

An Illustrated Care and Repair Manual for Boat Owners

PERCY BLANDFORD

David McKay Company, Inc.
New York

Copyright © 1977 by Percy Blandford

First published in Great Britain by Pelham Books Ltd.
under the title *Encyclopaedia of Small Craft Maintenance*

First American Edition 1979

ISBN: 0–679–51358–2

Library of Congress Catalog Number: 79–84216

10 9 8 7 6 5 4 3 2 1

MANUFACTURED IN THE UNITED STATES OF AMERICA

Introduction

To keep any boat in good condition there has to be regular maintenance. This can be done professionally and some jobs are better left to an expert, but much of the work needed to keep a boat in good condition can be done by the owner, even if he does not consider himself much of a craftsman. In fact, a large number of small craft owners get much of their enjoyment and satisfaction out of owning a boat by working on it to improve and maintain it. Carried to extremes this might mean they are always working on the boat and never using it, but there is a fine balance that most of us manage to maintain, so pleasurable maintenance can alternate with use of a boat that we know from personal involvement is in good condition.

In the not very distant past it was usual to regard part of the year as the boating season, then there was the ritual of laying up at the end of the season, followed next year by fitting out. Of course, there is something to be said for paying special attention to jobs on the boat at particular times, but for many boat owners the season has got longer so both ends meet and their little ship can never be considered completely out of commission.

With specific laying up and fitting out times, jobs tended to be left for these occasions, but modern usage makes maintenance more of an ongoing thing, to be done as needed and when circumstances permit. This is a more sensible approach. Many things that go wrong may be quite trivial at first, but if they are neglected they get worse and the repair job becomes bigger. 'A stitch in time saves nine' was a saying in square rigger days, but it is a worthwhile motto for any boat owner today.

There have been great changes in the materials and construction of small craft in recent years. For the thousands of years that man has gone afloat, wood has been the main material of construction. This has had to give way to glassfibre, particularly for quantity-produced craft. However, tradition dies hard and many owners still prefer wood. Glassfibre does not lend itself to one-off construction nor to amateur alterations and modifications. Wood has a feel and appearance more pleasing than glassfibre, metal or ferro-cement and it is used both for utility and effect by professional and amateur workers. Consequently, most readers of this book will be working in wood more than any other material.

Besides the changes in boat construction there has been a parallel revolution in fabric and rope. Gone – or almost gone – are the natural fibre canvases and ropes. Synthetic filaments give us stronger and more durable sail cloths and ropes for the many lines on board. Although some of the older working techniques are still applicable, there are many special points to watch when dealing with the newer materials. Instructions for knotting, splicing and repairing sails published not so long ago may be out of date. Even such things as glues and stoppings have changed for the better. Paints may look much the same, but their constitution is very different from traditional paints.

Most of these changes have not only improved boats, but have made maintenance easier, either by making parts more nearly maintenance-free or simplifying what work has to be done. Not that skill and care can be ignored, but even a professional boatbuilder no longer has to depend on the skills built up during a long apprenticeship. Both he and the amateur worker can do satisfactory work with less skill and often simple equipment.

Of course, this book takes into account all the modern aids to small craft maintenance, but there are many craft of traditional construction still in use, and likely to be for a long time. A well-built boat that is properly maintained can have an extremely long life. There is none of the early obsolescence found in cars. Because of this, a boat is a good investment and worth looking after.

With the book arranged in encyclopaedic manner, it is hoped that the reader will be able to find the subject he wants without difficulty. So far as possible closely related subjects come under one heading. There has had to be a balance between breaking maintenance down into a multitude of small items and lumping them together into too comprehensive a coverage. For instance, giving each knot a separate entry would have been tedious, so for any knot look under 'Knots'. Exceptions come where there is specialized maintenance required on an item that could have otherwise come under a collective heading, but it is hoped that ample cross-references will allow the reader to easily trace the information he needs. This is a book to dip into as well as one to provide specific information when needed, so casual reading will soon familiarize the reader with the layout. There has had to be a small amount of duplication of information to avoid too much reference from item to item, so what is needed will usually be found in one entry, but there are cross-references to related subjects or places where some additional information may be found.

We may consider that Americans speak English. True, we may understand each other on general subjects, but even then there are subtle differences, while in technical terms related to boating there are many completely different words with no immediately apparent comparison. Yachting in all its aspects is a very international thing. Much equipment and information passes both ways across the Atlantic and it is helpful to know alternative names. This book is written in English 'English', but there is a glossary at the beginning of the book summarizing the terms that are different.

It is hoped that readers will get as much enjoyment out of properly maintaining a boat as the author has, and that this book will be a means towards that end.

Percy W. Blandford

American and English terms

Although most boating terms are the same on both sides of the Atlantic there are some, mostly technical, that could lead to difficulties or misunderstandings. As boating equipment from one country is used in the other and this book may be read in many countries, it is hoped that the following lists of words (omitting many spelling differences) may help in knowing what the other man is saying:

English	American
Accelerator (used with resin)	Promoter
Aerial	Antenna
Aluminium	Aluminum
Anorak	Parka
Bracket	Brace
Centre of lateral resistance	Center of lateral plane
Clinker planking	Lapstrake planking
Coping saw	Scroll saw
Cotton wool	Batting
Countersunk screw	Flat head screw
Cramp	Clamp
Crocodile clip	Alligator clip
Curtain	Drape
Dismantle	Disassemble
Duffle bag	Tote bag
Earth wire	Ground wire
Electric fire or heater	Furnace
Englefield's clips	Brummel hooks
Eyelet	Grommet
Glassfibre	Fiberglass
G-cramp	C-clamp
Gripfast (barbed ring) nails	Anchorfast, or Stronghold nails
Groove	Dado
Jig saw	Saber saw

English	American
Kicking strap	Boom vang
Methylated spirit	Alcohol
Paraffin	Kerosene
Perspex	Plexiglass
Petrol	Gas, gasoline
Plait	Braid
Plastic wood	Wood dough
Press stud	Snap fastener or snap
Quay	Pier or wharf
Raised head screw	Oval head screw
Reinforced concrete	Ferro-cement
Rubbish or waste	Garbage or trash
Sacking or hessian	Burlap
Sacrificial plate	Electrolysis eliminator block
Silencer (in exhaust)	Muffler
Socket (electric)	Outlet or receptacle
Spanner, wrench	Wrench (never spanner)
Speedometer (mileometer)	Odometer
Tap	Faucet
Terminal (battery)	Post
Terylene	Dacron
Timber	Lumber
Toe strap	Hiking strap
Transfer (adhesive letter, etc.)	Decal
Valve (radio)	Tube
Ventilator	Cowl

A-bracket (Fig. 1)

Under the hull of many inboard boats
the shaft is supported forward of the
propeller with a bracket shaped like an
inverted A or with a single arm for a
small installation. Security of this is
important for smooth running. Check
the fixing bolts for tightness and corrosion. If replacements are needed they
should be of the same metal to avoid
electrolysis. Brackets are usually of a
bronze alloy compatible with the shaft.

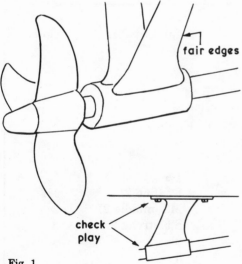

Fig. 1

The arms of the bracket may have
been damaged by hitting debris. Fair
them off with file and abrasive paper.
Check the shaft bearing for play in the
bracket. In many brackets the water-
lubricated bearing is easily replaced,
otherwise the bracket may have to be
relined or bushed.

see also ELECTROLYSIS.

Abrasives

A variety of abrasives are used to
smooth, clean and polish many materials. Normally filing, planing or other
working is followed by a coarse grit
abrasive and successively finer ones,
with all trace of one stage brushed or
wiped off before using a finer grade.
Power sanding has its uses, but final
sanding is best done by hand. Disc sanders will quickly remove material, but
leave curved marks. A belt sander is
better for work along wood grain, while
an orbital sander gives a good finish,
but is slow. For hand sanding, the
usual-size sheets are best broken into
four and wrapped around a cork, wood
or hard rubber block.

Powder abrasives are used to clear

corrosion off metals, take gloss off paint and for work on shaped parts that would be difficult with sheet abrasive. For metal carborundum, emery and similar abrasives may be used on a cloth with oil. Pumice powder may be used dry or wet on a cloth. Domestic scouring powders may be used the same way as pumice on wood, paint or varnish.

There is no such thing as sandpaper, although the term is still used. The modern equivalent is glasspaper. The particles of glass are held to the paper with a non-waterproof glue. The life of a sheet of glasspaper can be prolonged if it is heated to drive off any moisture in the glue.

The common abrasive for metals is emery, which may be on paper, but is more likely to be on cloth. It may have a non-waterproof glue and benefit from heating. It can be used with paraffin to prevent clogging.

Garnet is used instead of glass and this usually has a longer life on wood. It is found on sanding sheets for power tools as well as in sheets for hand work.

Aluminium oxide, silicon carbide and

ABRASIVES – comparative grades

Use	Numbered	Glass and	Emery
	grit	garnet paper	cloth
Finest finish	400		
	320		
	280		
Very fine on wood	240		
	220		
Finest commonly on wood	180	00 (flour)	0
	150	0	FF
Medium sanding	120	1	F
	100	1½	1
Usual first sanding	80	F2 (fine 2)	1½
	60	M2 (middle 2)	2
Rough sanding	50	S2 (strong 2)	3
	40	2½	4
	36	3	

other manufactured grits are used on 'wet and dry' paper. The name indicates a waterproof glue. Using these abrasives wet reduces clogging, particularly when using fine abrasives on glassfibre and hard-setting paints.

Steel wool is sometimes used as an abrasive, but there is a risk of tiny particles becoming embedded in wood grain, where they may rust in the damp conditions afloat and spoil appearance. Bronze wool as an alternative is made, but not easily obtained.

Metal and plastic polishes are really very fine abrasives in cleaning fluids.

The logical method of grading abrasives is by the size of the grit and this is done for 'wet and dry' and some other abrasives – the lower the number, the coarser the grit. Several other methods of grading are also used and approximate equivalents are shown in the table. Power sanding grades are generally coarser than the hand sanding grades that get the same results.

see also ALUMINIUM; PAINTING TOOLS; POLISHES; SANDING.

Adhesives

Except for a few cabin finishings, all adhesives used on a boat should be fully waterproof or have a very high resistance to water. The commonly available wood-to-wood adhesives are urea glues. The best known British makes are Cas-camite Waterproof' and 'Aerolite 306'. These are synthetic resins. With Aerolite 306 a powder is mixed with water to make a syrup. This is applied to one surface and a liquid hardener to the other. When the surfaces are brought into contact a chemical reaction takes place and the glue sets. With Cascamite Waterproof the hardener is also a powder mixed with the resin powder. When water is added, setting commences and the glue must be used in a short time. Some other glues of similar types are only available in commercial quantities. These glues are satisfactory on the exteriors of boats not kept afloat for long periods. They weaken after very prolonged immersion.

Resorcinol glue (Aerodux, Cascophen) has a greater water resistance.

Epoxy (Araldite) is the strongest and most waterproof glue, but because of its cost it is normally only available in small tubes. It will make a strong bond to plastics, metal and most materials, as well as wood, but the normal grade is slow-setting.

For melamine and other rigid plastics used for galley tops and similar applications, the impact adhesives are suitable. For canvas to canvas or wood, use thick rubber adhesive (Black Bostik). For plastic fabrics to themselves or to wood use plastic adhesive (Clear Bostik).

None of the usual adhesives can be used on foam insulation or buoyancy material, as they dissolve it. Special adhesives are available from poly-styrene manufacturers.

The single-pack PVA and similar woodworking adhesives have some water resistance and sufficient strength for many furniture applications, but they are not strong enough for boat building.

With all of the boat building wood-to-wood adhesives, the surfaces should be in close contact, but not clamped excessively tightly. If it is necessary to fill a gap, do not use glue alone, but mix in sawdust, otherwise the setting glue will craze and lack strength.

There are no common solvents or other ways of softening or reversing the process once a waterproof glue has set.

see also FRAMES AND TIMBERS; LAMINATING; SCARFING.

Adhesive tape

Not all self-adhesive tapes will stand up to damp conditions. Sellotape and com-parable stationery tapes are unsuitable for boat work. There are electrician's insulating tapes that are waterproof, but wider tapes of similar type are made which are intended for boat work. Some are unbacked plastic. Stronger tapes have fabric embedded in the plastic. These tapes will adhere to any dry surface, with the best grip if it is smooth. The grip is secure, but if the tape has to be peeled off it does not leave a mark.

Self-adhesive tape can be used for temporary repairs to a hull – several pieces may be overlapped to make up a width. It can be used to hold card to a hull when making a glassfibre repair. It can be used as a bandage for a tempor-ary repair to a cracked spar. It can be used on rigging to prevent sail chafe. A roll about 5 cm (2 in) wide is worth keeping on board.

Masking tape has a similar adhesive on a paper backing and is mainly used to limit a painted area.

see also MASKING TAPE.

Aluminium (Fig. 2)

Pure aluminium is not used afloat. Instead, an alloy with small quantities of other metals to give special qualities – in particular strength and resistance to corrosion by sea water – is used. Even with the correct alloys slight corrosion will occur – this is in the form of a white powder that can be removed with abra-sive paper. If there is deep pitting, as with aluminium parts of ex-car engines used in boats, that is a sign that the aluminium alloy is not sea-water resistant and should be replaced. Alter-native sea-water-resistant parts are available for some popular car engine conversions.

Equipment and complete boats built of the correct aluminium alloys do not require paint, except for appearance. If

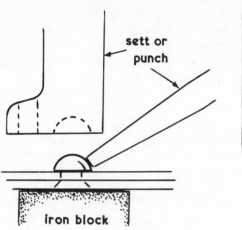

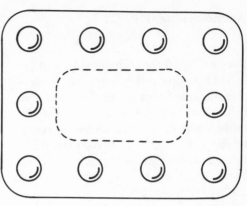

Fig. 2

polished aluminium becomes dull and scratched it can be revived with fine abrasive: 'wet and dry' paper or emery powder with oil for deep scratches; pumice powder and water for general dullness. Use these on a cloth by hand. Alternatively, use a polishing power-driven bonnet and a grade of polish intended for aluminium.

If aluminium is to be painted for the first time clean the surface with a solvent or degreaser and use the primer recommended by the paint manufacturer to precede the further coats. Ordinary primers do not bond well with untreated aluminium.

Many aluminium boats are assembled by riveting (see drawing). Leaks may sometimes be cured by tightening rivets, but be careful of damaging sur-

rounding surfaces. If a seam has to be sealed or a riveted patch repair made watertight there are jointing compounds available, but the resin intended for glassfibre can be used. Round off the corners of the patch and the cutaway damage.

A hole in aluminium can also be repaired with glassfibre in the same way as a car panel using plastic putty for small damage or mat and resin for a large hole. The area around the damage should be filed and roughened with abrasive paper, then the glassfibre allowed to overlap inside and project sufficiently on the outside for sanding level.

see also ABRASIVES; FASTENINGS; GLASSFIBRE.

Anchor cable (Fig. 3)

For small craft the anchor cable is likely to be fibre rope, but two or three metres of chain next to the anchor will improve holding as this keeps that end of the cable low to give a pull nearer horizontal. Both ends of the fibre rope should be spliced around metal thimbles and the chain attached to the rope and the anchor with shackles.

If the cable is natural fibre rope, open it at intervals. Blackness inside indicates rot, and the cable should be replaced. Synthetic fibre rope will not rot but may have suffered inside from abrasion by grit or sand. If there are many broken filaments, the rope should be suspect. Check externally for chafe at fairleads. Most cables are rarely used to their full extent, so turning end for end during fitting out will equalize wear and lengthen life. A much-used cable may be washed with fresh water and a mild detergent, followed by hosing and drying.

New chain is normally galvanized, but this will wear through where one link rubs on another. This is inevitable and some wear must be expected. However, if links have lost much of their thickness, the chain should be replaced. Usually the chain is considerably stronger than the rope, so some wear can be accepted, but a reduction to three-quarters thickness is about the limit.

Shackles in the cable system should be locked. If this is done by wiring, see that the wire passes through the shackle where it cannot be chafed.

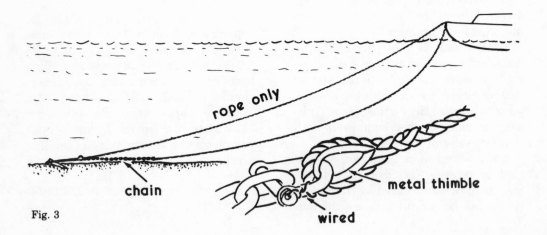

rope only

chain

metal thimble

wired

Fig. 3

Anchor chocks (Fig. 4)

If the anchor stows on deck, it should have a stowage that retains it and prevents it doing damage. How this is arranged depends on the anchor, but usually there are chocks fixed to the deck. Check them for security. If water has got below them, lift them to dry their undersides and the deck surface, otherwise rot may develop. Bed them down on jointing compound. Slots for flukes or other parts of the anchor should slope so water will run out. If there is a hollow which cannot be treated in this way, drill a diagonal drain hole.

An anchor may have to be taken from its stowage quickly, so it should not be fastened in place in a complicated way. A lanyard to an eyebolt may be positioned to tie down with a slip reef knot somewhere near the centre of the chock arrangement. If the rope cable does not stow elsewhere, it may be coiled down with the anchor on top and the lanyard through the centre of the coil. Lanyard ends should be sealed and whipped.

Anchors (Fig. 5)

There are a great many types of anchor, but all have one or more points intended to dig into the river- or sea-bed and a means of attaching a cable which gives

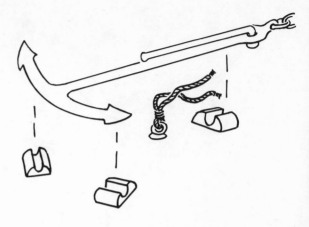

Fig. 4

a limited swing while the pull is at a low angle, but when the cable is hauled in the amount of pivoting reaches its limit and further pulling causes the point to dig its way to the surface. Maintenance is mainly concerned with checking that the anchor is still sound and that these functions can be performed.

There is no need for a knife-like edge or point, but if the flukes are badly worn, they may be filed sharper. Some flukes and the parts of plough anchors may have lost their shape and can be hammered back, using a rock as an anvil. Some anchor parts pivot on a peg which may get worn. It may be drilled or driven out and replaced.

Check a folding stock of a fisherman anchor, particularly for security of the means of locking in position and the strength of the little chain that retains it. If the stock is insecure and comes out

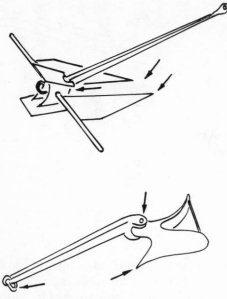

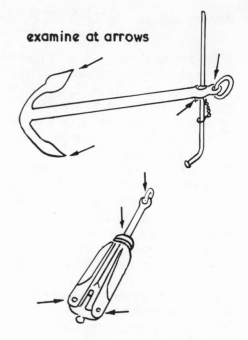

Fig. 5

of place the hold of the anchor is likely to fail. If there is a shackle at the anchor head, the first thing to wear is likely to be its pin. If this has happened, replace it. Rivet the screwed end of the shackle pin.

For an annual refit an anchor may be derusted and painted for the sake of appearance, but paint is unlikely to last long when the anchor is put into use.

Anti-fouling

The bottom of any boat afloat is attacked by marine growths and in some cases by marine creatures which attach themselves or bore into a wooden bottom. What will attack a bottom and how serious the effect will be depends on local conditions. Consequently, if anything is done to combat fouling, it should follow local advice. The problem is only acute if a boat is kept afloat for long periods. A boat that is normally kept ashore and can be washed or scrubbed after use should not need any special treatment and the paint used below the waterline can be the same as that used above it. Boats used in fresh water may gather weed, mostly near the waterline, and most of this can be removed with a long-handled scrubbing brush.

Anti-fouling paints are mostly expensive and their effective life may not be long. Tarlike black varnish and bitumastic paints are sometimes used. They are not true anti-foulings, but they provide a simple and cheaper treatment. Fouling occurs on hulls of all types, although borers will not enter anything but wood. Fouling on any hull can seriously affect speed or the power needed to push the hull through the water.

Many anti-fouling paints are only effective if they are immersed before they can dry and are then kept immersed. These 'soft' anti-fouling treatments give off a chemical which discourages fouling. Some treatments will withstand drying briefly between tides, but the most effective ones are best on craft always afloat. This type of anti-fouling may not be suitable for very fast craft.

Normal anti-fouling paint does not give a smooth surface, so is unacceptable for racing craft. For this purpose there are 'hard' anti-foulings, which give a finish as smooth as ordinary paint. They are not as effective at deterring fouling, but they are satisfactory if the bottom is cleaned down at intervals during the season. They do not depend on being kept immersed, so a 'hard' anti-fouling paint can be used on trailed boats that spend long periods out of the water.

There are simpler anti-fouling paints to deal with the lesser problems on inland waters. There is nothing to be gained by using an expensive seagoing anti-fouling paint on an inland cruiser.

Anti-fouling of any type is usually brushed on, but a roller can be used. It is also possible to spray, but this would have to be done with equipment more advanced than that available to most amateurs, and health precautions need to be taken as the fumes from many of the paints can be dangerous if inhaled. The makers recommend two coats for most types. Where immersion has to be within a certain time of application, the boat has to be located ready for launching and painting may have to be done to suit a tide time.

Some anti-foulings contain copper. As there would be a risk of electrolytic corrosion, these should not be used on steel or aluminium craft. Hard racing copper anti-fouling on racing craft can be burnished and polished.

The makers specify a recommended coverage which ensures an adequate coating. Do not brush out as in normal painting. A thin coat will not provide enough protection. The area needing greatest protection is from the waterline down for a short distance. Weed fouling is mainly in this area 'between wind and tide'. Fouling occurs when a boat is at rest. Moving through the water or the water moving past the stationary boat at only a low speed will be enough to prevent fouling. Fouling is much less in cold water than in hot conditions.

If anti-fouling is to be applied to a bottom that has been previously painted or has had a coat of anti-fouling which has ceased to be effective, follow the makers' instructions. In most cases, after cleaning off there should be a coat of a special primer or undercoat to seal the surface before putting on the anti-fouling. Those anti-foulings that depend on a chemical leaching out to kill fouling will gradually become thinner until none of the anti-fouling is left. There is then no doubt about when a new treatment is required. With others, however, appearance and an increasing need for scrubbing will show when new treatment is advisable. The majority of treatments may be expected to last a season in British waters.

To do their work anti-fouling treatments have to contain poisons which are harmful to eyes, skin and other parts of the body, so avoid contact with them and work in a well-ventilated place.

see also BOOT-TOPPING; KEELS; PAINT; PAINTING TOOLS.

Anti-theft devices

Most of the devices to make burglary of a cabin boat difficult or warn off intruders are battery operated to produce light and noise. If this lets you down, it is a negative investment. If it has a dry battery, it is advisable to replace the battery at least annually. If there is life in the old battery, it may have other uses. Efficiency of the system depends on clean contacts and good insulation. Terminals and connectors should be opened and scraped bright before reassembly. Using a waterproof spray on bare metal and any doubtful insulation will help maintain condition. The only real test is to try the system with a fake forced entry. It may be possible to connect a lamp instead of the noise-making device during the test to avoid unnecessary noise while adjustments are made, but performance of the complete system should finally be tested.

Security arrangements for an outboard motor or other moveable equipment may have been left undisturbed for a long time. Check the functioning of locks. Not all locks are intended for damp conditions. They may need oil to prevent rusting, as well as to ease their functioning. There are devices intended for household security that may have uses afloat. A catch that can only be operated inside may be used to limit the opening of a window. Locked chain may be used instead of rope for mooring or fastening oars in a dinghy.

Bailers (Fig. 6)

The traditional bowl-shaped bailer with a handle extending from the side may need refurbishing with varnish or paint on the handle and a check of the rivets holding the parts together. A plastic scoop-type bailer should be checked for breaks or splits. A ragged edge may be sanded, but cutting off a narrow strip will produce a new straight edge. Old and discarded plastic containers can be cut diagonally across to make good dinghy bailers, often with the container handle given a new use. A bailer ought to have a long lanyard, preferably spliced on to discourage undoing – even if a bailer made from a plastic container costs nothing, its value cannot be measured if lost overboard far from shore.

Balance of sails (Fig. 7)

Any sailing craft should carry a slight weather helm, so if it is left to its own devices it will turn into the wind and stop. In a small boat, where the disposition of the crew affects trim, fore and aft as well as athwartships, a satisfactory balance between sails and hull can be achieved by moving weights about. In a larger craft adjustment can be made by altering the keel surface (all of the underwater profile viewed from the side), possibly by moving ballast, or by adjusting the rig.

There are two terms to consider. The centre of effort of the sails is the point at which all the wind pressure may be assumed to be concentrated to get the same effect. With a triangular sail it is

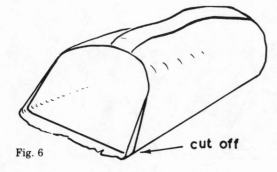

Fig. 6

cut off

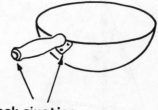

check riveting

the geometric centre (A). With several sails it is the centre of their combined areas (B). The centre of lateral resistance is the centre of the underwater profile (C). In both cases it is the vertical line the point is on that matters. Although positions can be found geometrically, in practice they move according to the attitude and speed of the boat, so theory can only go so far.

If a boat has lee helm (the tiller has to be pushed to leeward to keep the boat straight, or equivalent with a wheel) the centre of effort is too far forward in relation to the centre of lateral resis-

tance. Shifting ballast to get the hull further immersed forward may help. Raking the mast aft will move the centre of effort back (D). Reducing the size of a foresail (E) or even raising it on the forestay (F) will move the combined centre of effort a little aft.

If weather helm is excessive, the hull can be weighed down more aft. The mast can be raked forward, a larger foresail can be used, or the normal one set lower or further forward, if this is possible – all actions opposite to those for curing lee helm.

If these minor modifications do not

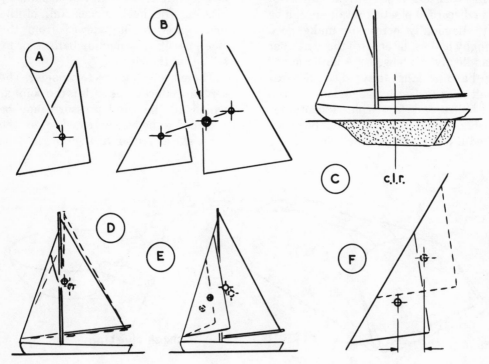

Fig. 7

22

cure the trouble, professional help may have to be called to alter sails, keel surface, size of rudder, location of outside ballast, or other structural alterations.

Excessive weather helm slows the boat. Lee helm can be anything between a nuisance or a danger as the boat would run off the wind in emergency and not stop.

Ballast

Loose ballast blocks made of lead need no special treatment, but iron blocks should be removed occasionally and painted. At one time tar, or one of its products, was used, but bitumastic paint is less messy. Check the support and security of the ballast. Thin strips of wood under the blocks will keep them clear of the hull. The blocks should be contained by strips of wood to prevent movement where structural parts of the hull do not hold them. Consider how the boat may heel or pitch, and restrain the ballast so it would not move at the most extreme angles. If there is a considerable amount of ballast in blocks of various sizes, make a sketch of their location before removing for painting, so they will be returned correctly.

Battens (sail)

Most main sails have battens to hold out the leech. Basic battens are usually of wood, but they may be plastic, glassfibre, metal or combinations of these materials. Edges and ends should be well rounded otherwise they may chafe stitches in the batten pockets, doing damage which may not be immediately apparent from the outside. Round off with file and abrasive paper. Wood battens should be varnished, then sanded again. If fixing is by cord through holes, see that there is no roughness in the holes.

If a batten warps, it can usually be cured by bending it the other way and leaving it wedged in this position for a period, until it will spring back straight and no further. If a batten breaks, a replacement is better than a repair. A glued repair will produce a local hard spot, which will cause uneven bending and may affect the shape of the sail. It is better to carry a spare. If the battens are of different lengths, let the spare match the longest, then it can be cut, if needed, to replace a shorter one. Even if the standard battens are of a sophisticated construction, a satisfactory spare may be homemade from wood.

Battery

It is important to keep a lead/acid battery fully charged, otherwise it deteriorates rapidly. It should also be topped up to the marked level. Unless acid is spilled, this should only be done with distilled water. A hydrometer can be used both for topping up and testing the state of charge by measuring the specific gravity of the acid. When acid is drawn up by squeezing the bulb, the float should indicate the state of charge by the mark where it breaks surface. This may be by a colour or by a figure indicating the specific gravity, which should be close to 1·250 if the cell is fully charged. Check each cell. If there is much discrepancy or acid is known to have been spilled, have the battery refilled and charged at a garage. If the engine is not used sufficiently to keep a battery charged, take it home and use a trickle charger. A battery that will not retain its charge is due for renewal.

Keep battery terminals clean by wire brushing and scraping. Check that connections to them are tight. Coat with a special anti-corrosion jelly or petroleum jelly (Vaseline). Protect the top of a battery from spray or dampness.

Lead/acid batteries used afloat are similar to those used in cars. Nickel-cadmium alkali batteries (Nife) do not deteriorate through being left uncharged and they will take a crash charge better, but they are more expensive and do not have as high an output per cell. The output from a single lead/acid cell is about 2 volts. From a nickel-cadmium cell it is about 1·4 volts. If a change is planned during servicing, a 12 volt lead/acid battery of six cells will have to be replaced with eight or nine nickel-cadmium cells.

Because batteries are heavy, they should be kept low in a boat, but they must be clear of bilge water. A tray will protect the batteries and prevent acid going into the bilges. A wooden box-like tray is suitable and this should be lined with rubber or be heavily pitched.

see also ENGINE ELECTRICAL SYSTEM; IGNITION SYSTEM; INBOARD ENGINES, PETROL; INBOARD PETROL ENGINE FAULTS.

Bell

A ship's bell may seem a bit of nostalgia on a small cruiser, as it will not be used for sounding time or changes of watch, but it does have a purpose in fog, so if there is a bell, it should be effective. To get the best note, the bell should swing freely. Check that the bolt or peg on which it swings is secure, but does not squeeze the lug on the bell. Similarly, the clapper should move freely. It is often swung on a hook loosely engaging with a ring in the bell. This is convenient if the clapper is to be removed when the boat is out of use, but to avoid loss overboard or elsewhere, a few turns of sail twine might 'mouse' the hook. Also, to preserve the tone of the bell, the clapper should be swung by something flexible and non-resonant, so do not fix a rigid handle. It is often an elaborately plaited bell rope, but the sound will be just as good with a plain cord or leather strap.

Bell metal is a form of brass. It may be plated, but otherwise will need polishing. Annual maintenance might include polishing on a power buff. A coat of lacquer may be applied to preserve the polish. It is unlikely to affect the tone of the bell noticeably.

Bilge pumps

The parts of any bilge pump most likely to give trouble are the valves. These are usually synthetic rubber (neoprene). Other parts of some pumps may also be of this material. Most pump manufacturers can supply a kit of replacement parts. This is worth having to service a much-used pump, although for many pumps new parts are easily cut from sheet material.

Some plunger-type pumps rely on the close fit of a piston in a cylinder. There may be one or more leather washers to replace, or caulking cotton wrapped around a grooved piston. Use cotton, not synthetic material, and soak it in grease, of the type used for the underwater gear of an outboard motor.

The suction side of the bilge pumping system must be airtight. Unsatisfactory pumping may be due to a rubber inlet hose that has become porous or to loose joints. Replace the hose with plastic and use tight hose clips at any joints. Obviously, leaks on the output side are a nuisance, but these would not affect the efficiency of the pump. New hose and clips here may also be needed. It does not matter how the hose runs on the output side, but avoid upward loops on the input side. These would cause air locks and make suction difficult. There must be a filter at the suction end of the hose. These are often too small. The combined cross-sectional area of all the holes in the filter should be at least twice the cross-sectional bore of the hose, to allow for up to half the holes being stopped by debris. Anything less may mean the pump working to less than capacity. A filter can be cleaned by running water through it the wrong way, followed by poking out anything remaining.

Some bilge pumping systems benefit from a non-return (clack) valve near the filter, particularly if the height the water has to be lifted is great, or the pump is a type that works with an intermittent action – an up-and-down stroke, instead of a continuous action. A simple flap valve is suitable and a unit combined with a filter may be bought.

see also LIMBER HOLES.

Blocks

Blocks may be anything from a sheave on a plain bearing in a plain wood or metal shell to many sheaves with roller bearings in a stainless steel and plastic shell. Satisfactory lubrication of a plain block can usually only be done by removing the pin which forms the axle, often by knocking it out. Clean off rust or corrosion and use graphited grease, which will have a longer life than plain oil. With a more modern block, the bearing should be packed with the grease or oil recommended by the makers. A plastic sheave may not require lubricating.

If a block is wood, it may be varnished. Metal binding should be cleaned and polished. If there is a rope strop it may be due for renewal, or the seizing between block and thimble made again with new line. The plastic composition used for some blocks needs no special treatment, except for worn edges to be filed and sanded smooth.

If a block is worn to the point where the sheave wobbles or there is a space at its side where the rope might jam, it is usually advisable to replace it as a satisfactory repair may be difficult. This is particularly so if it is out of reach when sailing.

Boarding ladder

If a ladder is used for swimmers or for climbing from a dinghy, the most important check during maintenance is for security. For a brief period anyone using it is solely dependent on it, and it must not give way.

If the main construction is wood, check joints and see that they are secure. Bolts may need tightening. Screw holes may have to be plugged and the screws redriven. If a glued joint has loosened, yet cannot be dismantled for cleaning out and regluing, it may be possible to fix a glued block in the angle under the tread or a metal bracket can be screwed there. A tie rod right across under a tread and through the sides, as seen in household ladders, can have its ends screwed with nuts or riveted over washers.

There are many ways of hooking on a ladder, but they usually involve metal plates screwed to the deck and hooked pieces to engage with them on the ladder. Check all fastenings, clean out recesses in the plates and clean and polish all metalwork.

Has the ladder marked the side of the boat? If the hull is to be repainted, now may be the time to fix padding behind the ladder. This can be a sponge rubber strip stuck on. A suitable type is used for sealing car doors.

Varnished wood may look attractive, but it does not provide a good foothold when climbing on board. Metal treads are unsuitable for bare feet. Non-slip self-adhesive strip sold for deck use, can be stuck on treads.

The boarding ladder should have a regular and secure stowage on board. This may also need attention. If the ladder has been refurbished its stowage hooks or brackets may benefit from padding so they do not mark the new varnish or allow the ladder to swing and get damaged.

Boathook

A boathook has to pull or push something too far away to reach by hand. The first concern is to ensure that it is reliable. If the shaft is wood, ash is the best choice, although it is not very durable. It has a better resistance to breaking when bent than any other British wood. The head usually fits over the tapered end of the shaft and is attached by screws. If the head is loose, remove the screws, check that the tapered end is sound, then turn it to a new position in the socket and drive the screws again. Cut off a doubtful end and repoint the remainder.

Varnish or paint is needed to protect the wood, but it may be better to leave the end untreated for a better grip. A hole drilled across the end can take a loop of rope to slip over the wrist. If the boathook shaft is an aluminium tube, its ends should be plugged with wood or plastic, so it will float if dropped overboard. Grip can be improved by binding with electrician's tape or by using a plastic sleeve, softened in hot water and slipped over to shrink on as it cools.

Many boathooks have sharp points for pushing and pulling. These are good for dealing with a rough bank or trees, but not with another boat or finished woodwork ashore. A hook with ball ends is better then, so a second boathook may be advisable.

Boom crutch

There are several types of support used for the boom on craft larger than dinghies. Whatever is used must provide a definite support that can be trusted. Some rely on standing in position and may lift if the boat rolls. A peg on a lanyard may be taken through a hole to lock parts together. Even with the feet of the crutch secure, the boom may lift out. There should be a lanyard or other arrangement to keep it in place.

Some crutches may damage the boom. Leather or plastic padding may be added. In any case, all parts of the crutch should be rounded. During annual maintenance the crutch should be painted or varnished. It may be worthwhile marking it with the name of the yacht, in case it gets lost overboard.

Boot-topping

This is the name given to a band of paint along or just above the waterline, usually a different colour from the paint above the water and the anti-fouling below. This part which is sometimes wet and sometimes dry can suffer badly from fouling with 'grass' or weed. The paint used for boot-topping should be a 'hard' anti-fouling, of a type that can be scrubbed. Two coats are needed.

The band should follow the true waterline and not be too wide – 5 cm (2 in) is the most for an average small yacht. Masking tape may be used to give a good line against the topside paint, but if a soft anti-fouling is used for the bottom, tape should not be stuck on as this may lift the anti-fouling. Follow the makers' instructions about undercoat.

see also ANTI-FOULING; PAINT; PAINTING TOOLS.

Bottled gas

Gas provides the means of cooking and of some lighting in many small cabin craft. It is convenient, efficient and safe if properly installed and used, but it is potentially dangerous, so regular maintenance is important. The gas commonly used is butane, but this will freeze at about the same temperature as water. If that happens no more gas will flow until the gas cylinder has been warmed. Propane is the alternative. Its freezing point is very much lower than any temperature likely to be experienced by the average yachtsman, so propane gas will always flow. Propane is not quite as hot as butane, but both are much hotter than mains gas ashore. Butane and propane can be used for the same appliances, but they have different unions at the cylinder and the regulator, which reduces gas pressure, is different. Maintenance is the same whichever gas is used.

Bottled gas is heavy and this is the main cause of danger. If gas leaks and gets into the bilges, it cannot be removed merely by ventilating. A spark or flame will ignite it and with the spread gas, the whole interior of the boat will very rapidly be engulfed in flames. Installation and maintenance should be directed towards the prevention of leakage. If gas has leaked into the bottom of a boat, it should be removed very carefully.

Make sure no more can leak in the same way. Ventilate as much as possible. Avoid anything metallic that might cause a spark. Walk about in rubber shoes or bare feet, not hard shoes. Do not use any electrical installation – certainly not a bilge pump. Obviously, do not smoke or use a flame for any purpose. Use a plastic bucket to bail gas from the bilges and tip it over the side. If you can smell the contents of a bucket, you know you are succeeding.

If there is any way of blowing into the bilges, do this, but do not suck gas out. If a vacuum cleaner can be set to blow, it has possibilities, providing the actual motor, which may spark, is above deck; but if it is set to suck, that motor spark may ignite the gas. Fanning with card may also disperse the gas. Arrange for the gas to be driven from one end and out at the other end of the boat. Only after the gas has gone should the boat be ventilated as normal. Getting your nose into the bilges is the only satisfactory way to check.

Gas containers should be stowed on deck if possible or in another open place where escaping gas will disperse overboard. If a cylinder is to go into a compartment this should be gas-tight and made of non-inflammable material, with the only access through the top. At the bottom there should be a vent pipe through the side of the boat, so this means the stowage must be high enough above the waterline for the vent to be clear of water.

To check stowage, see that there are no breaks in the structure of the compartment, that the vent is clear and the gas cylinder lifts in and out without risk of fouling or damaging pipes. Some regulators depend on a fibre washer to keep them gas-tight when tightened on to the cylinder. Replace this occasionally. Although some caravan installations use a synthetic rubber hose to connect the regulator to the system, it is better not to have any flexible pipes in a boat system. Instead, it is usually possible to give the copper pipe a few turns to give it spring and flexibility and join it directly to the regulator. If the way the system is arranged requires more flexibility at the regulator, there is armoured hose with screwed end connections that can be used, in as short a length as practicable.

In the usual system gas is carried by copper pipes, with screw connectors or unions. When a union is tightened, a sleeve on the pipe is squeezed. This should make a gas-tight joint dry, but there is a special Calor jointing compound that can be used. If a union is unscrewed during maintenance, this jointing compound should be used when the joint is remade.

Check for leaks by using a soapy solution with a brush. If there is a leak the gas will cause bubbles. Usually, tightening the union with a spanner is all that is needed. Be careful of straining the whole junction. Hold the connector with another tool when using a spanner.

Gas taps are not usually troublesome, but if one is found to leak it may have to be dismantled and cleaned before reassembly. Gas light fittings tend to become dirty and sooty. Dismantle and remove obvious dirt with a cloth or brush. Do not poke a jet. Blow through it, preferably with compressed air, which may come from a tyre foot pump.

Gas cooker fittings can usually be removed easily. Top parts that support pans lift off and the burners may be found to come away without the use of tools, leaving the gas jets as fixtures. With a much-used cooker it may be advisable to wash out the burners with hot water and soda to remove accumulations of dirt and soot. Holes in the metal burners may be poked out, but make sure that anything pushed inwards can be shaken out. A cooker or a light burns a mixture of gas and air. Check the position of any air adjustment before dismantling for servicing. If the maximum air is used, the mixture burns most efficiently and economically. Observation of the flame or light will show when the best adjustment has been made.

If a gas refrigerator is fitted in a boat, check the maker's instructions before doing any servicing. The method of working and the need for a pilot jet means careful attention if any alterations or adjustments are made, otherwise there is a risk of leaks or explosions due to accumulated gas.

In some boats where gas is only used for cooking, a gas cylinder fixes directly below a two-burner or other hotplate. Maintenance is similar to a cooker working from a remote cylinder. When the gas cylinder is to be changed, it is advisable to take the whole unit out of the cabin, as a small leak during the fitting of a new cylinder cannot be avoided.

If gas is used for heating, the fire should be fixed and ideally should be of the type which has air ducted in and out, so the actual heating is by a heat exchanger and the jets do not consume air from the cabin. This type is best left alone if it is functioning correctly. If a gas fire of the open type is used, the burners should be dismantled and cleaned in the same way as a cooker.

If gas is burned for lighting, heating or cooking, it draws oxygen from the air and emits poisonous gases. Adequate ventilation is important. If there is a circulation of air in the cabin there is no risk. A ventilator over a cooker aids air circulation as well as taking away cooking smells. During maintenance, see that there are air inlets and exits which cannot be blocked, for any enclosed space where gas is burned. Another effect of gas burning is to increase condensation, which may be alleviated in several ways, but can only be cured by ventilation.

The products of combustion will leave a deposit on paintwork, reflectors and anything else above a cooker or light. A domestic cleaner used on paintwork occasionally will avoid too great a build-up that will need more drastic treatment later. Similarly, metal polish on reflectors will restore their appearance and improve the effect of the light.

see also CONDENSATION; FIREFIGHTING EQUIPMENT; HEATERS; VENTILATION.

Brass

Common brass is an alloy of copper and zinc. It is not a good choice for use afloat as salt causes loss of zinc and weakening of the alloy, but some boat equipment is brass. It may be protected with

30

paint, but for a natural finish it can be polished and coated with a clear lacquer (e.g. nail varnish). Alternatively, frequent polishing will provide protection as well as improve appearance.

Brass is produced in several ways – rolled brass in sheet or wire is strong enough to accept bending and shaping; extruded brass in special sections or made into bolts is too brittle to bend much. Brass-work hardens. Tool work on it, particularly hammering, hardens it and makes it more brittle. If this happens to rolled brass, it can be annealed by heating to redness and allowing to cool.

Brazing (Fig. 8)

Brazing, or hard soldering, is a method of bonding metals together by melting spelter in the joint. It is similar in some ways to soft soldering, but it produces a much stronger joint, although not as strong as welding. Common spelter is a form of brass, being an alloy of copper and zinc. Its melting point is lower than that of copper alone or most of the bronze alloys, but it may not be lower than ordinary brass, so there would be a risk of the object being brazed also melting. For use where this risk exists there is silver solder, which is spelter with a small amount of silver included, which has the effect of reducing the melting point far enough to make it safe to use on brass. Brazing is unsuitable for aluminium and its alloys, but is suitable for most other metals and alloys, although some cast and extruded alloys may suffer if heated excessively.

It is necessary to raise the temperature of the parts being brazed to a red heat. It need only be a very dull red for silver solder, but a more pronounced red is needed to make spelter flow. This must be allowed for when considering brazing, as some article may suffer if heated that much. It is more suitable for making new items, where metal parts are joined before other work is done on them.

Spelter and silver solder are obtainable in wire or sheet form. Pieces of scrap sheet brass may be suitable for use as spelter. As with soft soldering, there has to be a flux to cover the joint and prevent the hot metal oxidizing as well as help the spelter to flow. There are prepared fluxes that can be bought, but borax powder is commonly used, either applied as a powder or mixed with water as a paste. In any case, the flux melts and forms a glasslike film over the metal.

Heat comes from a blowlamp, which may be gas or paraffin, with a round controllable flame. As considerable heat may be needed if the metal is bulky, it is important to conserve the available heat. A metal tray of coke can be used or there may be firebricks. In any case, see that there is nothing nearby that could be damaged by flame or heat.

The meeting surfaces should be absolutely clean. Spelter does not flow as readily into close joints as soft solder, so there is some advantage in letting them be open slightly towards one side (A). If the part being built-up is hollow and the flame can be got inside, a good joint is usually easier to make from the inside (B). If a thing is being made from sheet metal, there may have to be some restriction to prevent it distorting as it gets hot. Iron wire can be used (C), as it has a high enough melting point to be unlikely to give way.

A piece of stout iron wire with its end flattened is useful as a spatula (D). Plenty of flux should be put on the joint. Some of it may bubble away as heat is applied, so be ready to put on more with the spatula. Small pieces of spelter can be put along the joint with the flux. If so, be ready with the spatula to push back any that are lifted off by bubbling flux.

The alternative is to have a length of spelter ready to touch on the joint when the temperature is judged to be sufficient.

Start by heating around the joint, so heat flows towards it and the flux melts without being blown away. When the flux has flowed over the surface, point the flame more directly at the joint, but move it so as to get an even spread of heat. As the heat builds up sufficiently, the spelter will melt. It may not flow as readily as soft solder, so use the end of the spatula, red hot and dipped in flux to spread the spelter where it is needed or to add more. Where the assembly is suitable, as in a T-joint, the spelter or silver solder can be drawn through a joint by using its tendency to flow towards the hottest part. Put flux on both sides, but spelter on one side. Use some general heating all round, but as brazing heat is reached, concentrate on

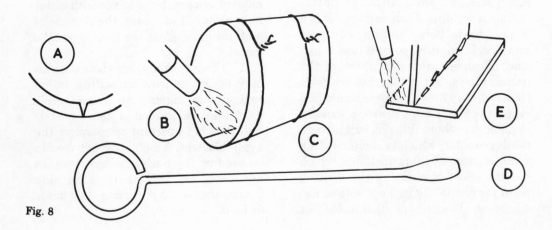

Fig. 8

the side without the spelter (E) and watch for the yellow line as the spelter comes through.

Let any brazed joint cool naturally and keep the parts held without risk of moving until well below brazing temperature. Final cooling can be in water, for anything except tool steel. Because of the heat involved the hardening and tempering of tool steel will be affected by brazing. Cooling naturally without water after brazing will leave the steel soft and annealed. Rehardening and tempering would be needed to bring a tool back into use. Heating to redness anneals copper and any alloy in which it is used. This applies whether it is cooled quickly or slowly. In making some boat fittings this may be an advantage, as internal stresses will be removed. However, the part will be softer and more ductile than before heating. It may regain some hardness with age, but the only sure way to reharden is to work the metal, which may not be practicable with some things. A piece of sheet brass or other copper alloy may be hammered. If a strip that has been brazed is needed as a spring, hammering it on an iron block will make it very hard and springy.

see also SOLDERING, SOFT.

Buoyancy, reserve (Fig. 9)

Many small craft, particularly sailing dinghies, which are liable to capsize, need reserve buoyancy. If a boat does not have inherent buoyancy, i.e. is not made of wood or other buoyant material, then sufficient reserve buoyancy should be added to prevent sinking. How much is needed depends on how high the waterlogged boat is expected to float. In the case of a sailing dinghy this is preferably with the top of the centreboard case above water, otherwise bailing is difficult or impossible.

Reserve buoyancy placed anywhere in the boat has value, but having it high is preferable to having it low. Buoyancy only between skins in the bottom of a boat may make righting more difficult than if it is under the decks. It should also be spread so trim fore and aft is reasonably level no matter which way up the boat is. A boat that is down by the bow or stern, due to much more buoyancy one end than the other, may be very difficult to right and bail.

All of this should be considered when inspecting or re-arranging reserve buoyancy. Beware of adding excessive buoyancy, as the boat may then float so high when it turns over that the windage will make it travel so fast downwind that it could be taken into trouble and anyone in the water parted from it could not catch up.

If reserve buoyancy is in bags, inflate them and check for tell-tale bubbles when immersed in water. Patching can be done with a repair outfit for tyres or air beds, if the makers do not supply a suitable kit. Some synthetic rubber

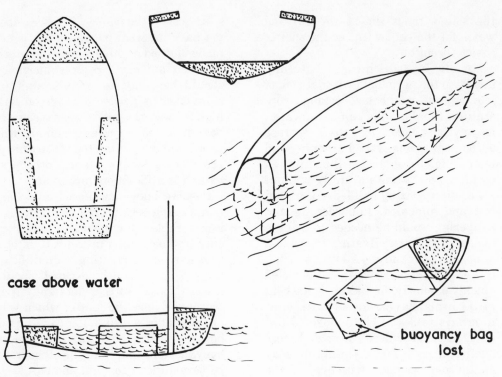

case above water

buoyancy bag
lost

Fig. 9

requires a special adhesive.

A buoyancy bag that comes out during a capsize can be hazardous. If there are eyeletted tabs for securing ropes, or straps provided for fixing in place, see that these are still tightly fitted. A strap or rope that goes around a bag or across an opening under a deck or thwart is better than any attachment that relies on something bonded to the skin of the bag.

If there is any sign of chafe on a bag, it may be patched although it has not worn through. Examine the part of the boat that has caused the chafe. If nothing can be done about smoothing this or removing the cause of chaffing, padding may be fixed there.

If the boat has built-in buoyancy compartments, each will probably have a drain plug. Water in any quantity will be obvious because it can be heard. If a small amount drains out, the particular case must be considered. A little mois-

34

ture inside may be acceptable. If the compartment has an inspection panel it may be possible to look inside and see light at a weak spot that needs attention.

Glued joints of a plywood buoyancy compartment may have broken due to flexing of the hull. New glue may suffer in the same way, as the normal wood glue sets hard and brittle. It may be better to go around the joints with glassfibre tape and resin, but all paint or varnish must be removed so the resin bonds to bare wood. For an emergency repair self-adhesive plastic tape can be used around the seams. If such a repair is made to a surface which has been painted, the repair can be made permanent by painting over the tape, particularly if it is the type of tape that incorporates fabric.

Buoyancy compartments that are glassfibre in a glassfibre boat are unlikely to give trouble if they have been properly fitted. If there are any leaks, they can be sealed with tape and resin as described for plywood. If there are actual holes punctured in either type of compartment, the repair may be similar to that described for hulls, although small damage in plywood or glassfibre buoyancy compartments may be filled with resin and bits of glassfibre matt, then sanded level after setting and painted over.

The main problem with plastic foam buoyancy is securing it. Slabs of buoyant foam material under thwarts and decks puts buoyancy in the best place and does not take up otherwise useful space. Some adhesives attack the material and dissolve it, so they cannot be used. The adhesives used with some foam household ceiling tiles is not very strong and may not withstand damp conditions.

As most solid plastic foam material does not stand up well to knocks, it is worthwhile enclosing it in a polythene sheet, which can be heat-sealed or merely wrapped with seams against the deck or thwart. This is held in place with a casing or straps of plastic, fabric or light metal, screwed in place. Another way is to use adhesive for the foam directly to the structure above, then put polythene sheeting around the block and fix this to a wood thwart with tacks driven up through strips of thin plywood.

Foaming in position has possibilities, but care is needed as it can get out of hand. Two parts are brought together and immediately foam of a great many times the original bulk of the constituents is produced. Nothing can stop it and the process goes on until a certain amount of foam has been produced. If it is in a restricted space, which it fills before foaming has completed, something may burst or give way. If this is kept in mind and the maker's instructions read and followed, the result can be excellent.

Foaming in this way into an open-ended space will do no damage. It might be the forward part of a dinghy with a foredeck open towards the centre of the boat. This does not restrict foaming and an estimated amount can be directed into place and its aft surface left or trimmed level. If foaming is to be into what was an air compartment, there must be an outlet for surplus foam, as well as an inlet, even if this means cutting through a panel and fitting a cover later.

Foam-filling a compartment does ensure that even if the compartment has leaks there is no room inside for water. If a buoyancy compartment has reached the stage where there are doubts about it and any repair is also considered of doubtful effect, foaming into it is worthwhile. Air provides buoyancy. With plastic foam it is air in the multitude of little cells that provides buoyancy. The foam itself is not buoyant. Consequently, a certain volume of foam is not as buoyant as the same volume of air. However, the loss of buoyancy due to using foam instead of air only is very slight and for practical purposes can usually be ignored.

If the boat being worked on is a class sailing dinghy, there will almost certainly be class rules about buoyancy. Any maintenance work involving changes in the buoyancy arrangements should only be done after checking that the rules permit them.

The only satisfactory test of reserve buoyancy provisions is to capsize and/or fill the boat with water while it is in a good depth of water. Some class rules specify how this test is to be made and how frequently it should be carried out. For other boats try the effect of various loadings and no loading with the boat in various attitudes and degrees of righting and capsize. Check the effect of climbing on board and of bailing from in the water or after getting on board. This may show what variations there might be in the amount and disposition of reserve buoyancy.

see also GLASSFIBRE; PERSONAL BUOYANCY; PLYWOOD REPAIRS.

Buoys

A light buoy may be carried on board for use with the anchor, there may be a buoy on a line used for hauling a mooring chain on board or there may be a larger buoy that remains afloat and to which the boat is moored. The older type of metal canister buoy needs checking for leaks. If this is due to rusting through, the buoy should be discarded. It may be possible to solder or braze a hole. Epoxy glue can be used to stick on a patch.

If the buoy is made of an expanded plastic, this should be checked for cracking and breaking. If there is no casing, it may be possible to bind it around with cord. A hollow plastic buoy that relies on air for buoyancy may have a hole sealed by melting the edges with a soldering bit, but for most of these plastics there is no satisfactory adhesive for a patch. Self-adhesive waterproof tape will make a temporary repair.

If a metal or plastic can is used as a buoy, the cap should be screwed on to jointing compound. If the handle is used to attach a line, see that it is securely moulded in or is otherwise integral with the can. As this sort of improvised buoy could sink if punctured, it may be advisable to use cans in pairs to give reserve buoyancy in case of accident.

Besides buoyancy any buoy needs secure fastenings above and below. If there is failure at the underwater connection, the cable may not be recovered. As well as the cable connection to the bottom of a buoy there may be a line carried around to the top eye or shackle as extra security. A large eye at the top that can be grabbed by a boathook is always worth having. Painting a buoy fluorescent orange gives it maximum visibility. It may be worthwhile painting the name of the ship on the buoy. If it is a mooring buoy that someone else may use while you are away, an indication of the size of your craft may make it less likely that a craft too big for it may be put temporarily on your mooring.

Canvas (Fig. 10)

This is a rather loosely-applied term and many modern synthetic materials are probably better described as cloth or fabric. Canvas is woven, with the lengthwise threads called 'warp' and those across called 'weft', and the manufactured edge where the weft threads turn back called the selvedge. Some traditional canvas has a coloured 'selvedge strip' parallel with the selvedge as a guide for seaming.

Some older canvas was graded by number, but a more usual method is by weight per square metre before proofing, if any. Water and rot proofing increases weight and causes shrinkage, so cloth described as 90 cm (36 in) width may be less than 86 cm (35 in) in fact. Synthetic fibre cloths are graded in the same way, but there is no shrinkage problem.

Canvas may be made of many natural fibres, but cotton is commonest, with flax for heavy coarse material. Synthetic cloth may be polyester (e.g. Terylene; Dacron) or nylon for boat work, but other synthetic fibres are used. Cotton and other natural fibres are liable to absorb water and then rot. Treatment with proofing solutions can give a resistance to water absorption and rot, but this may not last long and treatment again will be required at intervals. Polyester is unaffected by water and does not rot. Nylon does not rot, but can absorb a small amount of water. Natural fibre cloth may stretch and distort. Polyester is very stable and unlikely to alter size or shape. Nylon is elastic. It is little used afloat except for spinnakers. Other sails are nearly always polyester. It is unusual for a modern sail to be cotton. Some heavier cotton canvas is used for awnings, dodgers and similar things, although these may also be synthetic.

Grades of polyester sail cloth are in fractions of an ounce from 1 oz to 6 oz on an average small yacht. Cotton canvas would be about twice the weight for comparable uses – between 6 oz and 15 oz for screens and similar purposes.

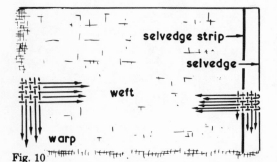

Fig. 10

Metric equivalents are in grams per square metre.

A cut edge will fray, if left untreated. Using pinking scissors to cut a zigzag edge reduces this tendency, but it is usual to turn under any cut edge when making seams or putting on a patch. Synthetic fibres will melt when heated and this property is used to heat-seal edges, which can then be used without turning under. Sufficient heat comes from an electric soldering bit. After cutting with scissors or knife, the hot bit run along the edge will melt the cut fibres together. Alternatively, file the copper bit to a knife edge and use that to cut and seal the edge in one action.

see also CANVAS REPAIRS; PRESERVATIVES; ROT; SAIL CARE.

Canvas repairs (Fig. 11)

If a sewing machine is available, it can be employed for most canvas repairs, particularly if it does a zigzag stitch. However, much canvas is too thick for a domestic sewing machine and repairs afloat may have to be done by hand in any case. The methods are the same, whether dealing with natural or synthetic fibre cloth, except that the thread used should match the cloth. Cotton or hemp thread or 'sail twine' is easier to use, but it would not have the same durability as using synthetic thread on synthetic cloth.

Hand sewing of light cloth might be done with a domestic needle, but for thicker canvas use a sail needle. This is triangular behind the point (A), to push a sufficient gap for the eye end and the thread. Needle sizes are denoted by a gauge number, with half sizes. For normal needs, a few needles between 14 and 17 gauge will do. Protect them from rust by storing in a container. The needle is pushed with a palm (B), which is worn over the hand and the iron block engages with the needle so the whole hand can push.

Nearly all sewing is done with double thread and the ends are included under the first few stitches. At the end of a row of stitches the needle is taken back under a few stitches to give a similar finish. If more thread is to be joined in a long seam, the new and old ends are twisted together and laid under the next few stitches. Natural fibre thread is pulled through beeswax or a piece of candle before use. This lays down hairs on the thread, waterproofs it and helps it to stay put during stitching. Synthetic thread does not have to be waxed, but wax helps hold stitches as they are formed, as the thread is otherwise very slippery.

A hole may be darned with over-and-under threads both ways. Heat will make a hole in polyester or nylon, so a cigarette end on a sail will make a hole. A rip, either straight or right-angled, is more likely. It should be repaired with-

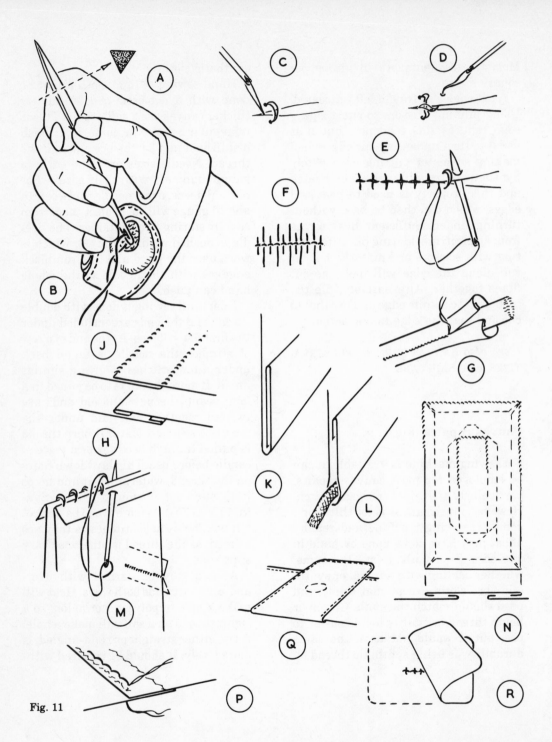

Fig. 11

out delay, otherwise the damage may spread.

A small rip can be drawn together with close herringbone stitches, with no need for a patch. Use doubled thread and knot the ends together. Pass the needle up through the left of the rip and bring it over and down through the near side, with the point coming up in the rip on the left of the stitch (C). Take the needle over the stitch, into the rip and up through the far side again (D). This is a complete herringbone stitch. Come down through the near side and up on the left of the crossing, and so on (E).

The work is shown open for clarity, but when dealing with a rip, make the stitches close to each other and vary their length so they pick up different parts of the cloth (F).

If torn edges come under strain, but a patch is to be put over them, some of the load can be taken off the patch if wide herringbone stitches are used to draw the edges together. Another use for herringboning is in covering a spar or rail with canvas. Turn under the canvas edges and draw the folds together with herringbone stitches (G). The tension of the canvas can be adjusted by varying the amount turned under as stitching proceeds.

If two pieces of canvas have to be joined by hand stitching, the best joint is a flat seam. The selvedge of the cloth can be used flat. Synthetic cloth that is heat sealed may be used flat. Otherwise turn under a cut edge (H). Any folds should be rubbed down with a knife handle or piece of wood. Sew with a simple over and over stitch along one edge, then turn the work over and do the other edge (J). Five or six stitches to the inch should give good results.

If an edge has to be strengthened, it is tabled. If eyelets or other fittings are to go through the tabling, let the turned-under part be the full width (K). Sew in the same way as for one edge of a flat seam. If a draw string is to go through the tabling, turn under only a small amount (L).

A simpler and quicker method of joining cloths is to use a round seam. Fold the edges inwards and bring them together inside out, and sew over the folds (M). Pull the cloths straight afterwards. This is best regarded as an emergency method of joining, except it has possibilities for joining-in the bottom of a bag, which is sewn inside-out, then turned to bring the raw edges inside.

A patch is put on in the same way as making a flat seam. The damage is trimmed to a neat shape and a patch made to overlap all round. If edges are heat-sealed there is no need to turn them, otherwise turn the hole edges outwards and the patch edges inwards (N). A similar patch may be put over herringboning.

Check existing stitching, particularly on synthetic materials, as the stitches do not pull below the surface in the same way as they do on natural fibre materials. This means they are more likely to chafe. Broken stitches can pull and the seam loosen each side of the initial damage. New machine stitching can be done over or alongside the old stitching. It is inadvisable to pull out old stitching, unless a complete seam is to be resewn. Hand stitching to reinforce may be up and down from one or both sides (P).

If an eyelet or other attachment pulls out, it is unlikely that a replacement can be fitted securely without reinforcing the canvas. Sometimes an oversize eyelet may be used, but the canvas edges will not take another one the same size as before. Sew on a patch. If it is at an edge, let the patch wrap over (Q).

There are adhesives that will join fabric to fabric or to other materials, but they will mark the cloth and cannot be treated as temporary repair materials. If a canvas patch is stuck on, it should be intended to remain. Adhesive is necessary if the repair has to be waterproof. It may be in addition to sewing, or in place of it. There is no universal adhesive for fabric. Natural fibre may be stuck with black rubber cement (Black Bostik). For synthetic fibres there are clear adhesives, but not all are suitable for all materials. Plastic-coated fabric usually has PVC on cotton or nylon woven cloth. A tear in this can be herringboned and a patch of similar material stuck over. Follow the maker's instructions – usually the adhesive surfaces have to be left some time before bringing together.

Round off the corners of the patch to reduce the risk of coming away (R). Lower the patch from one side, so as to avoid air bubbles. Most of these adhesives do not allow adjustment after they come together.

see also CANVAS; EYELETS; GROMMETS; REEFING GEAR; SAIL CARE.

Carvel planking (Fig. 12)

Conventional carvel planking has flush planks with caulking between, but there are other methods of flush planking that are mostly repaired and maintained in the same way. A good surface can be sanded and revarnished in the normal way. If there are blemishes they can be filled with stopping and sanded level. As carvel planking is usually comparatively thick, it may be possible to cut away a badly chafed part, only deep enough to get below the damage and inset a new piece of wood (A). Let it be too thick and work it level after the glue has set.

If the damage is right through, the simplest repair is to clean the edges of the hole reasonably true and fill with glassfibre and resin, then paint over (B). If the repair has to match the existing planking, the damage should be cut out as far as midway between frames. Joint covers are made to fit inside (C), then a new piece of plank made to fit closely. It

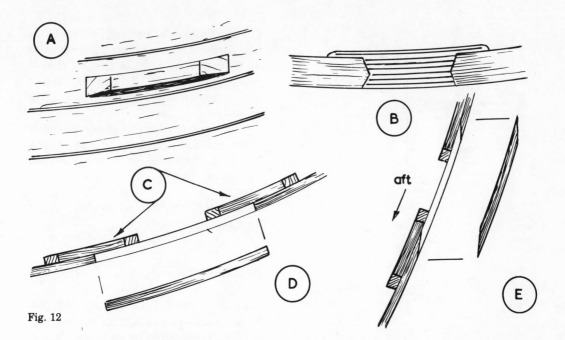

Fig. 12

can have simple butt joints (D), but is better scarfed to long angles (E) with the outside feather edges aft. Close fitting of a renewed piece of plank needs careful and skilful work and may be better left to an expert.

see also CAULKING; GLASSFIBRE.

Caulking (Fig. 13)

At one time many carvel-built yachts had their fore-and-aft plank joints filled with caulking. Modern craft are not built this way, but there are working boats and craft converted from them that employ caulking. Caulking is also used between deck planks, even when today these are only thin planks laid over plywood.

Caulking has to fill the joint and make it waterproof, but it has to have some flexibility to allow for the expansion and contraction of the planks. It is important that caulking should be under an even tension. Excessive caulking in one place may cause opening and leaking elsewhere. This should be kept in mind when replacing caulking. Usually it is wisest to make the replacement for a greater distance than appears necessary, so any build-up can be gradual.

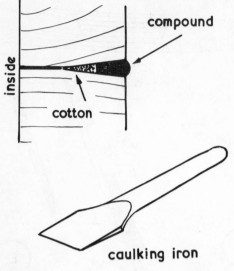

compound

inside

cotton

caulking iron

Fig. 13

The edges of planks to be caulked, whether hull or deck, meet when first assembled, but are made to give a slight v to the outsides. In traditional caulking, strands of cotton are driven into the bottom of the V with a caulking iron like a thin, blunt, cold chisel. If cotton has to be replaced, the new strands are introduced in loose loops – not stretched along the seam.

The cotton used to be covered by a variety of compounds, some of which had to be heated and poured. For modern caulking there are synthetic compounds of a fibrous nature that are easier to apply. They are pressed into the joint and will retain enough flexibility. In a repair the only problem is judg-

ing the amount of pressure to be put on the cotton and caulking. This needs to be driven tight, but not so tight that it goes right through. An examination of surrounding caulking will show what is needed.

The synthetic caulking compound is more suitable for stopping leaks below the waterline than the stoppings used elsewhere in the boat.

see also CARVEL PLANKING; STOPPINGS.

Centre and dagger boards (Fig. 14)

A wooden centre or dagger board should have an underwater section similar to a rudder. The bottom tends to get chafed and rough in use. Reshape it, but make sure any water has dried out before revarnishing or painting. If the pivot hole of a centreboard has worn, repair it in the way suggested for the blade of a lifting rudder.

The inside of a wooden case should be protected, preferably with a waterproof paint or mastic. This can be applied with a cloth pad over a flat board (A). In wooden construction there may be several places where water can enter joints or end grain in a wooden hull (B) and even if waterproof paint or other finish is not used for the full depth of the inside of a case, enough should be used to come above the joints. One way of ensuring adequate penetration is to close the bot-

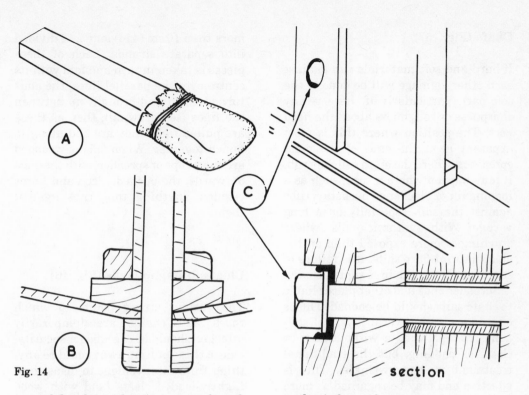

Fig. 14

tom of the slot with a temporary board, then pour in the liquid from the top and allow it time to soak in before removing the board to drain off surplus.

A metal centreboard puts a heavy load on its pivot. Check the bolt for wear and replace if necessary. A galvanized centreboard may need no special treatment, but other metal boards may be painted, possibly with the same paint as the bottom of the boat.

Check the full up-and-down functioning of a centreboard. If it relies on the forward end of the slot to act as a stop in the down position, check this for wear

and reinforce if necessary.

If there are leaks at the pivot bolt, jointing compound may cure them. Larger washers will give a greater coverage for the compound. It may be possible to reinforce the sides of a case and let the washers in, to give the best sealing with jointing compound (C). If there can be a tube on the pivot bolt, that will prevent the tightening of the bolt pulling the case sides in and allow maximum tightening, preferably with a locknut.

see also KEELS; RUDDER.

Chafe (Fig. 15)

If hard and soft materials rub against each other, damage will be done to the soft part, particularly if there is any sharpness or roughness about the hard part. The position where this is most apparent is at the ends of the mast spreaders, where the main sail may rub. It may happen where a rope, such as a topping lift or slackened backstay, rubs against the sail, especially on a long voyage. With synthetic sails, where stitching is more exposed than on the older natural fibre sails, it is failure of stitching that is the first sign of chafe.

Spreader ends and other places liable to chafe sails should be padded. This is often done with several layers of self-adhesive tape, with or without foam or cloth for padding, but the traditional treatment is 'baggywrinkle'. This is effective and may be regarded as more 'boaty' on spreaders or stays.

Baggywrinkle uses up oddments of rope and discarded rope that are unfit for other uses. Two pieces of light line are stretched parallel, or one piece is doubled back to get the same effect. Three-strand rope is cut into lengths no

more than 10 cm (4 in) long and divided into separate strands. Each of these pieces is taken in turn and laid with its centre over the parallel lines, the ends turned down and brought up between the lines (see drawing), then as these are pulled tight they are slid along to bunch together. When this is wrapped around a rope or spreader, with the ends outwards, the opened yarns and fibres cushion anything that rubs against them.

Cleats, bitts, bollards (Fig. 16)

The various strong points to which ropes and chains are temporarily attached should be checked for security. One of these pulling away could be anything from inconvenient to disastrous. Lightly-loaded cleats held with wood screws may have screw holes plugged and screws redriven. It is sometimes possible to use a longer screw with a larger diameter. In wood of doubtful holding power, a mixture of epoxy glue and sawdust may be put in the hole and the screw driven into it, so it bonds

Fig. 15

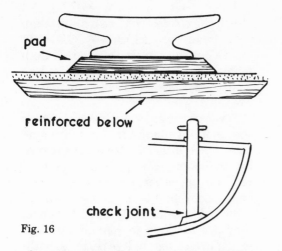

pad

reinforced below

check joint →

Fig. 16

when the glue has set. As it will be impossible to withdraw the screw, this should not be done where dismantling may be needed.

Where a considerable load has to be taken, see that this is not just localized, but that reinforcing pieces spread the load to other parts of the boat structure. Where there are through fastenings, check their anchorage for movement, holes elongating or pulling in.

Where there is a samson post or other strong point passing through, the load levers on its foot. Check that this is strongly held to the hog or other part of the boat.

Wood is stronger than rope, but not as strong as chain. If bitts or a post are used for both, check for roughness that might damage rope. Clean up with a file and abrasive. If a metal rod is passed through a wooden post, check that it cannot come out. If it is only a push fit

and it has loosened, it may be possible to drill a thin hole through the wood into its centre for a fine nail to go through.

Clinker planking (Fig. 17)

A traditionally-built boat with planks overlapping does not normally have any glue or stopping in the joints, but it depends on a close fit, backed up by fastenings and the fact that the wood swells in water. It is unwise to attempt to cure leaks by filling them as this may interfere with the swelling of the wood at that point and cause a joint to open elsewhere.

Ideally, an old clinker boat should not be allowed to dry out. However, it may be necessary to haul it out to dry for painting or repairs. In this case, it should be allowed to 'take up' gradually, preferably by being put on a slipway where it floats at first for only an hour or so each tide, then it can be moved to where it floats longer as joints close. First leakage of a very old boat may be alarming, but joints will close after two weeks or more of gradual soaking.

If a joint is so wide that it cannot be expected to close, use a flexible stopping that never completely hardens, so any surplus will squeeze out as the wood swells and not prevent natural movement. However, if it is an overlapping nailed joint, tighten the fastenings before putting in stopping, as described below for nail sickness.

The clinker method of construction dates from long before the use of engines and a hull may suffer from the vibration set up by a power plant. Fastenings are usually copper nails driven through roves and riveted inside. Vibration may cause a slight stretching of the nails and consequent leakage, the effect being called 'nail sickness'.

Nails can be tightened by holding an iron block or a hammer against the head while a light ball pane hammer is used inside to tap around the riveted head on the rove inside. Do this gently, or the nail will bend in the wood and straighten again later so the leak returns. It may be necessary to work progressively as a row of nails is tightened, going back over earlier nails again as the joint closes.

If the trouble is due to nails pulling into the wood, it may be better to replace them. On the inside, centre-punch the riveted end and drill through the spread head so the rove falls off. Punch out the remains of the nail from inside. Check its thickness and replace it with a thicker nail and matching rove.

Towards the ends of clinker planking the adjoining planks are brought to the same level, either by bevelled edges or by one plank fitting into a tapered recess in the other. Fastenings to stem or transom may be by copper nails or screws. If copper nails have loosened, they are unlikely to remain tight for long if driven again. It is better to withdraw them, if possible to grip their heads with pincers, and replace them with barbed-ring nails or screws. If they cannot be withdrawn, drive the new fastenings alongside them, but drill slightly undersize first to reduce the risk of splitting the ends of the planks. Hammer the old fastenings tight and punch their heads below the surface if there is enough thickness of wood.

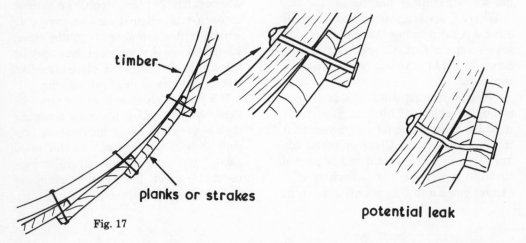

timber

planks or strakes

potential leak

Fig. 17

Cover with stopping.

Clinker planking may be painted or varnished with conventional finishes. Because of the expansion and contractions of the planks, do not use any two-pot synthetic finish that sets hard, as this will crack. There are flexible underwater finishes intended particularly for clinker hulls. For inland use and salt water not liable to cause much trouble with weed or borers, black varnish and other tarlike products are used. Bitumastic paint may also be used as a cheaper finish than anti-fouling paint. Many of these finishes will penetrate or span gaps and reduce leaks in old hulls. Once used, they cannot be painted over successfully with conventional paints, so black varnish, bitumastic paints and similar preparations must follow on in subsequent maintenance.

It is possible to sheath a clinker hull. Normal glassfibre and resin may not conform very well to the overlapping bands of clinker planking and make a good grip, then gaps between sheath and wood may harbour moisture and encourage rot. Nylon (Cascover) and the adhesive supplied with it, is probably better for clinker. A hull to be sheathed needs to be cleaned off to bare wood, preferably mechanically, as a chemical stripper may clog the pores of the wood. As much as possible of paint and other things that have penetrated the pores of the grain should be removed, so the adhesive or resin can penetrate. Edges of planks should be rounded. Any sheathing should be from gunwale around to gunwale, so there is an unbroken cover around the whole boat. Sheathing only to just above the waterline is unsatisfactory, as water may get behind the sheathing and the edge cannot be expected to remain close for long.

see also FASTENINGS; KNEES; TINGLES.

Compass

If a steering compass has been properly installed and corrected, there is little maintenance needed. More important than the compass itself is the arrangement of anything with magnetic properties around it. If gear on board is re-arranged, care is needed if any of it could affect the magnetic action of the compass. This applies to electrical gear as well as anything containing iron or steel.

If there is doubt about the compass, it could be tested on a known bearing, possibly obtained from a chart, or from landmarks identified from a map if testing on inland waters. If a second compass is available, this may be used to compare bearings, but the two instruments should be kept far apart. When using a hand bearing or other portable compass, be careful that there is nothing nearby that will affect it – a belt buckle may cause trouble. If a compass is at fault, it should be repaired by an expert.

Compasses need to be viewed clearly. Use window cleaning material on a glass cover, but not on plastic. Clear plastic may be washed with detergent and water. If it has dulled, use metal polish gently. Brass binnacles are often lacquered. If not, they can be brightened with metal polish. If lacquer has worn, it can be cleaned off with amyl acetate (e.g. nail varnish remover), then the brass polished again and fresh lacquer applied.

Condensation

Condensation is the deposit of excess moisture in the air on a surface. If there is a considerable difference in the temperature each side of a cabin or hull skin or window, condensation is aggravated. Insulation may minimize this but, like double glazing, is unusual on a boat. Condensation is more apparent on a glossy surface that on a matt one.

Condensation in a cabin is due to it being lived in. The human breath gives out a considerable amount of moisture. Cooking produces more. Lighting and heating with a flame adds to the problem.

The only complete cure to the condensation problem is ventilation to the point where the air circulating inside is one with the air outside. As this amounts to living outdoors, it is unacceptable and some condensation is inevitable.

Living with condensation means doing everything possible to minimize its effect. Gloss paint will attract condensation. Even better than matt paint is covering with fabric or a foam plastic. There are special anti-condensation coverings that can be fixed either in sheet form or as thick, porous, paint-like plastic. These are particularly suitable under the cabin head to prevent condensation drips. Similar materials can be used on the inside walls of the cabin. Curtains of thicker material than usual also reduce the problem. Some condensation on windows is inevitable. There should be a grooved lip in the lower part of the window frame to catch the moisture, preferably with a means of letting it run away.

There can be considerable condensation under bedding, particularly if a dinette makes into a bunk and there is a glossy plastic table top. This should be covered with several layers of newspaper, which are discarded next morning. Holes in the bunk top under the mattress reduce the problem.

It may be understandable that attempts are made to cut out draughts, particularly during the night, but it is important for condensation considerations as well as other reasons, that there is adequate ventilation. If attempts are made to minimize the problem of condensation during maintenance, ventilators should be strategically placed so air can enter the cabin low down at several points and be allowed out through high ventilators. It is important that these inlet and outlet points should be of a type that cannot easily be sealed by an occupant trying to make the cabin cosy.

see also BOTTLED GAS; VENTILATION.

Corrosion

All metals corrode when in contact with many gases and liquids, but in some cases the amount of corrosion is negligible. The more pure the metal, the less will be the corrosion. Commercial metals are usually very impure. Dampness, and particularly salt-laden dampness, can cause rapid corrosion, so certain particularly vulnerable metals should be avoided on a boat or be given protective treatment. Iron and steel will rust. Pure iron is less seriously attacked. Corrosion of brass and other yellow alloys is in the form of a green powder. Aluminium, if it is not in the form of a salt-water resistant alloy, corrodes with a white powder and soon becomes pitted.

Steel tools kept afloat should be kept in a metal or plastic box (a wooden box attracts and holds moisture). Silica gel, in the form of crystals or as impregnated paper, may be kept with the tools to attract moisture away from them. The tools may be coated with grease or oil. Petroleum jelly (Vaseline) is less messy than lubricant.

Some iron and steel items are galvanized. This is a coating of zinc which gives temporary protection. It should be further protected with paint. Platings of various sorts also give protection, but they are usually porous and corrosion can only be kept in check by frequent polishing. Common brass (copper/zinc alloy) does not last long in a salty atmosphere. Besides corrosion of the surface, zinc is lost and the metal becomes brittle.

There are several bronzes which have been alloyed so the effect of salt water is negligible and some stainless steels are also unaffected. Aluminium is alloyed in many ways. Some of these alloys may be just as seriously affected as common aluminium, but there are salt-water-resistant aluminium alloys with a very good resistance to corrosion.

Rust-inhibiting fluids can be used to prevent the further progress of rust and one of these can be used under paint. If paint is applied directly to iron or steel with any trace of rust, corrosion will continue and stains will show through the paint.

see also FASTENINGS.

Davits

When a dinghy is slung by davits they form levers which put a load much greater than the weight of the dinghy on their attachment points. Maintenance involves a careful inspection of these places, particularly of fastenings pulling, brackets distorting or other signs of strain. Blocks, tackle, ropes and cleats should be checked. Lubricate moving parts. Replace doubtful rope. If there is a canvas sling to take the weight of the dinghy when raised, check this and its attachments. If the dinghy lowers on to chocks, check their padding. Paint or revarnish wood and renew padding if necessary. Be particularly careful if the dinghy hangs over the stern. A falling dinghy could be hazardous.

Decks (Fig. 18)

On some craft leaks from the deck are a more serious problem than the possibility of leaks through the hull, so decks should be kept tight. Larger older craft had teak decks with thick planks and caulking between. The caulking was a marine glue (not to be confused with adhesive) that was poured hot. If such a deck has to be repaired, old caulking should be scraped out and more poured in, but an alternative is a plastic caulking compound.

More recent decks with the same appearance are made with thin planks laid over plywood. They may be caulked again for the sake of appearance, but the plywood provides waterproofing. Teak should only be treated by scrubbing, but its appearance may be improved by wiping with a special teak oil.

If a plywood deck leaks, it must be at the joints. With the wood dry, obvious spaces may be filled with a glue and sawdust mixture. If the opening seems to be due to the working of the boat, it may be better to press in a flexible jointing compound.

A plywood or other surface may be painted, using a special non-slip deck paint. There are also plastic compounds to paint on that build up a safe thick surface that will cover cracks. Decks of glassfibre craft are often moulded with certain areas given a non-slip surface, while other parts are glossy. If further non-slip areas are needed there are self-adhesive strips that can be fixed on. Any paint on a glassfibre deck should be of a type that suits the material.

52

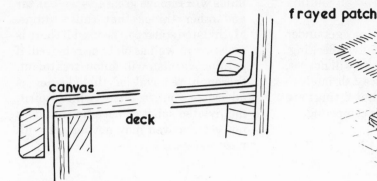

canvas

deck

frayed patch

Fig. 18

Canvas makes a safe-footed covering for a wooden deck. It may have been laid dry or on paint. Usually, where the canvas meets the base of a cabin wall etc., the edges are turned up a little and secured with quarter-round beading. At the gunwale and other edges the canvas goes over so water runs off. A sound canvas deck may only need repainting, but look for signs of rot where it goes under fittings or other places where water may be trapped. Rotted canvas should be cut away and patched. Damaged parts may also be patched.

To fix a patch to a painted canvas deck, scrape away the paint until the canvas fibres are exposed. Trim away the damage and allow for a patch that will overlap some way. Thin canvas may be frayed at the edges so it blends into the surface. With thicker canvas it is better to turn under the edges, rubbing the creases down tight. Use adhesive under the patch and tack around

the edges fairly closely. When the adhesive has set, paint the patch and the surrounding area.

A much-painted canvas deck may develop cracks in the paint layer. It is unwise to attempt to remove the paint with a stripper, as this may affect the canvas. A sealing compound may be worked into the cracks before applying more paint, but at this stage it may be better to use one of the thicker brushing plastic compounds.

There are embossed PVC plastic materials, such as Trakmark, used as deck coverings. This material is laid on bare wood and held down with an impact adhesive. If covering has lifted, use the recommended impact adhesive. Coat both surfaces and leave until apparently dry before pressing together. As the material shrinks a little with age there may be open joints where pieces butt. This cannot be made good by filling and the best treatment is a thin

53

metal moulding held down on jointing compound with screws.

As with canvas, water may get under fittings attached over PVC decking. Although the deck covering will not rot, moisture may find its way through to rot wood below, so see that fittings are bedded down on jointing compound.

see also FOOT RAILS; PAINT.

Degreasing

There are special degreasing fluids that can be used for removing oil and grease from the engine and other mechanical parts. For other things much can be done by washing with warm water and domestic detergent. White spirit can be used to remove grease from many things. Paraffin has a similar effect, but is more trouble to remove itself. Petrol will dissolve grease and has the advantage of any excess evaporating, but obviously needs care in use.

White spirit may be used to remove any residue of grease from the release agent on glassfibre or the natural oil from teak before gluing. Dry cleaning

fluids will remove grease as well as tar and other things that cause stains. Methylated spirit can be used if there is moisture as well as oil to be removed. If paint or varnish will follow treatment, thorough removal of the cleaner is advisable, but a little white spirit, methylated spirit or paraffin that does not get removed may not matter with most paints.

Desiccator

A drying agent is useful with any equipment that will suffer from moisture. This draws moisture to itself. There are silica gel crystals and special impregnated paper that will do this. When the desiccator becomes saturated it can be dried and used again. As the atmosphere in a cabin boat is often moist, desiccators can be put with electrical gear that might be affected by damp and some may be put with tools or other steel things that might rust. Check the desiccators periodically, and even if not fully saturated, dry out with heat before replacing them.

see also TOOL KIT.

Electrolysis

When two dissimilar metals are close together in salt water, an electrical action takes place between them and one will be eaten away. Because of this it is important that underwater fittings should have fastenings that are the same metal, if possible. It is sometimes impossible to avoid dissimilar metals being in the vicinity of each other, particularly around stern gear. In these circumstances a sacrificial plate or block may be fixed to the hull. This is usually mainly zinc and it becomes eaten away instead of the damage being done to vital equipment. This eating away may not be very quick, but the block should be inspected periodically and replaced when most of it has gone, so there is no risk of damage to boat parts.

In the list opposite the metal nearer the anodic end of the scale will be eaten away if it is in salt water near another metal. The further the metals are apart in the list, the more pronounced will be the effect.

see also A-BRACKET.

Anodic	Magnesium
	Zinc
	Galvanized steel
	Cadmium
	Aluminium
	Mild steel
	Cast iron
	Stainless steel, 13% chrome
	Solder
	Stainless steel, 18–8
	Lead
	Tin
	Manganese bronze
Cathodic	Brass
	Copper
	Silicon bronze
	Nickel
	Other stainless steels

Engine electrical system

An inboard engine may be started by a raised handle and an outboard engine may be started with a cord, but electric starting is usual as an alternative on some engines and as the only means of starting larger engines. The starter motor is usually arranged to drive by a

55

pinion that moves along a shaft to engage with teeth on a flywheel, then disengages when the engine starts. Electricity usually comes from the same battery as is used for ignition. Switching is via a solenoid where light current through the starter switch draws a plunger by magnetism to enable a heavy current to flow from the battery to the motor.

Maintenance is mainly seeing that the battery is fully charged and able to operate the motor. If hand starting is available, its use may allow the battery to cope with the needs of the spark plugs when it may not also be able to operate the starter. The starter motor on a boat engine is less liable to be clogged with dirt than the one on a car engine, but it should be cleaned occasionally and the shaft on which the pinion slides lubricated. If there are grease points, these should be attended to, but sparingly.

The battery may be charged by a generator driven by the engine. This is usual for an inboard engine, but for a few outboard engines where the battery is only used for starting and ignition is by magneto, the battery may have to be charged elsewhere. The usual charging method is via a dynamo driven by a belt from the engine. The same belt may also drive a water pump. An alternator is a less common and more recent alternative to a dynamo. The dynamo produces direct current (DC), which is what is wanted for battery charging. An alternator produces alternating current (AC)

and this has to be changed to DC via a rectifier, but an alternator can produce more current at low speeds so is better at charging the battery when the engine is idling. A voltage regulator combined with a cut-out controls charging and prevents the battery discharging through the generator.

Servicing is mainly concerned with seeing that the generator is working and its belt is tight enough to drive it without being over-tight. If there are lubrication points, these should be attended to sparingly. In a boat where the engine does not get much use or is run for long periods at slow speeds, the usual dynamo may not be able to keep the battery charged. In that case it should be taken ashore and either charged at home with a trickle charger or charged professionally with more advanced equipment. Leaving a battery in a partly charged state will cause it to deteriorate. This is particularly important if the same battery is used for lighting or other purposes as well as for the engine.

see also BATTERY; FUEL SYSTEM; IGNITION SYSTEM; INBOARD MOTORS, PETROL; INBOARD PETROL ENGINE FAULTS.

Eyelets (Fig. 19)

An eyelet is usually brass and in two parts. Single-part eyelets are for leatherworking and are not suitable for

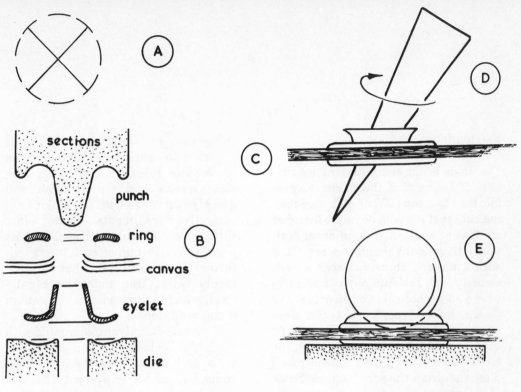

Fig. 19

use on canvas. Eyelets are best fitted with a matching punch and die. Grip is obtained by including canvas in the closing of the eyelet, so it is better to cut a cross in the canvas (A) than to punch a hole of the eyelet size, then the canvas edges will be pushed up the tubular part of the eyelet and gripped.

Rest the tubular part of the eyelet on the die, press the canvas over it and put the ring over that (B). Hold the ring down and hammer the punch in to spread the tubular part over the ring (C). A light blow with the flat of the hammer gives the maximum grip.

If a punch and die are unavailable, spreading of the tube may be started by rolling a spike around (D). A steel ball can follow (E). The ball pane of a hammer can be used, then the flat of the hammer. This may not produce as perfect a circle as a punch and die, but the eyelet should be secure.

If an eyelet pulls out, the canvas will be damaged so another one of the same size cannot be fitted. A larger eyelet may be used, or the canvas patched to take another of the same size.

see also CANVAS REPAIRS; GROMMETS.

Fairleads

The name is apt and maintenance consists of seeing that the fitting gives a fair lead to a rope. Wear on a side may indicate that it would do its job better at a different angle or in a different position. If there is any roughness, smooth it with a file and abrasive paper. Check security of fastenings, particularly where an anchor cable or mooring rope passes. Bolts through are better than wood screws. If wood screws have to be used and they have loosened, plug the holes with wood or a fibre or plastic wall plug and drive the screw again. Some plastic sheet fairleads may have worn to the point of needing replacement. Check them for cracks.

A fairlead may benefit from being raised. A piece of wood, larger than the base of the fairlead and with its edges rounded, will keep a rope from rubbing the deck or gunwale. On a light glassfibre deck or cabin top it can be bolted through to a similar block below to give stiffness.

Fastenings (Fig. 20)

All fastenings used on a boat should be salt-water resistant, even if it is expected to spend most of its life on fresh water. It is unwise to use common steel screws and nails, which will quickly rust, even with the majority of protective treatments. Some older fittings were of iron, which generates its own protective film of rust, to prevent further corrosion, but what is commonly called iron today is actually steel, which will rapidly deteriorate in damp conditions.

Steel may be galvanized (coated with zinc). This delays rust and galvanized nails and screws have been used on boats, but are better avoided. This also applies to cadmium and other platings on steel, although fastenings treated in this way may have some success ashore and might have a place in cabin fittings.

Brass has some use afloat and may be satisfactory on inland waters, but salt water or atmosphere causes a loss of zinc from the alloy, leaving screws and other fastenings in a weak state. Not everything described as stainless steel is immune to attack by salt water, so make sure that stainless steel fastenings are of a steel intended for marine use. There are several alloys described as bronzes that are used for fastenings and have good salt-water resistance. There are some suitable aluminium

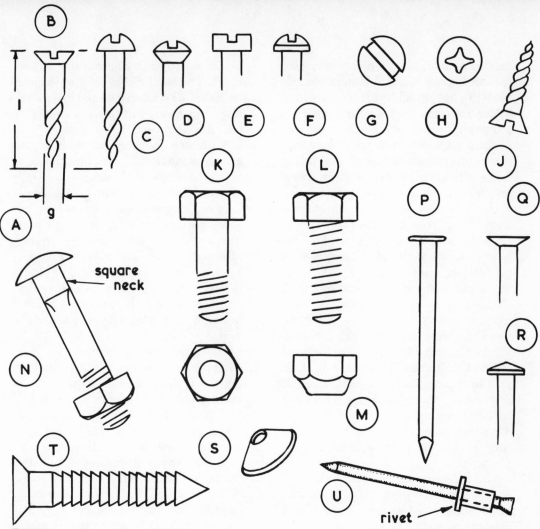

Fig. 20

alloys used for fastenings, but these are commoner in America than in Britain. Copper is a soft metal with good resistance to corrosion. It is used for boat nails, but not other fastenings. If a fastening is to go through metal, it should be a similar metal. In a salty atmosphere, electrolysis may set up between some dissimilar metals, and one metal will waste away.

Wood screws are described by their length from the surface and by a gauge size (A). Except for the smallest sizes, only even number gauge sizes are commonly available. Unless otherwise specified screw heads are countersunk (flat) (B), but round heads (C) may look better on some surfaces and fittings, although raised (oval) heads (D) are neat through metal fittings. Some large screws may have pan or cheese heads (E) or fillister heads (F). A large screw may also have a square head for use with a spanner, as well as a slot for a screwdriver. Normal screws have a slot for a flat screwdriver (G), but Phillips heads (H) were intended for quantity production work, and they are now being found in other applications.

There are several types of self-tapping screws, intended to drive like wood screws into metal. They can usually be identified by a thread to the head (J). As they have to be steel to do their job, they are liable to rust, even if plated, so are best avoided, but they are sometimes convenient for such things as an attachment to a metal mast, when they should be painted or otherwise protected.

The difference between a bolt (K) and a metal-thread screw (L) is in the length of thread, which goes almost to the head in a screw. Heads can be in any of the forms shown for wood screws, but are commonly hexagonal to take a spanner. Besides plain nuts there are several types of self-locking nuts, usually distinguished by an extension containing the frictional locking arrangement (M).

For some purposes it is convenient to have a head that grips the wood, possi-

bly in a situation where a tool cannot reach. The bolt for this purpose is sometimes called a coach bolt and has a shallow snap head, with a square neck to pull into the wood (N).

Nails are described by their length and by a gauge thickness (not the same gauge as screws), although some nails may only be available in one gauge per length. Common heads are flat (P), but there are countersunk (Q) and diamond heads (R). A nail may be round, although copper boat nails are usually square. They are used in clinker planking with roves. A rove (S) is a conical copper washer with a hole that needs a hollow punch to force it over the end of a nail.

There are bronze barbed ring nails (Gripfast, Anchorfast) with rings having a sawtooth cross-section to resist pulling out (T). They are made in several gauge thicknesses for each length. Avoid the thinnest gauges as they may bend and break when driven.

Rivets are not often needed, but they can be bought with one prepared round or countersunk head, then the other head is formed by hammering. Pop riveting has some use in places where only one side can be reached, as with an attachment to a hollow metal mast. The rivet is hollow and supplied on a shaft or mandrel (U). This is gripped in a tool which pulls the enlarged end back against the far side of the rivet to spread it, then the mandrel breaks off. The rivet is usually aluminium alloy. The mandrel is steel and the remaining broken end may rust and cause stains.

There are special fasteners intended for home use in making attachments to panels, where a screw is driven and the device expands on the other side. Some of these may have uses in cabins, but many are liable to rust. There are some plastic versions where a sleeve expands, and these are better. Wall plugs (Rawlplug) of the fibre or plastic type have some uses, particularly where a screw has lost its grip in wood and a plug can be inserted to provide a new hold.

see also ALUMINIUM; CLINKER PLANKING; CORROSION; FRAMES AND TIMBERS; KNEES; MASTS; SPARS; TINGLES.

Fenders (Fig. 21)

A boat has to be protected against damage to itself and from damaging whatever it comes against. What comes between usually suffers in the process. Consequently fendering or fend-offs, whether fixed to the boat or hung over the side, need frequent attention and occasional replacement.

Wood rubbing strips may be at gunwale level or lower down and quarter rubbing strips will protect the transom corner as the stern swings (A). The more the strips project, the better will be the protection of the hull, but considera-

tions of appearance limit how thick they may be. Hanging fenders may be used with wood rubbing strips, but they are not always in the right place and the wood will become chafed.

A chafed wood fender may have to be scraped or planed, but obviously much reduction of size has to be avoided. A Surform tool used in both directions will remove most roughness, but damping the wood after the first treatment will raise splinters and fibres that bent or stayed down. Follow by sanding. In a bad case, a section may have to be replaced, but join in with a tapered splice with its outside pointing aft (B). Screws driven from outside should be counterbored and their heads covered with plugs (C). If screws are driven from inside, particularly through glassfibre, have large washers under the screw head. Bed a new piece of rubbing strip in resin to prevent the entry of water and the possible onset of rot.

A hanging fender that gets caught between the boat and something solid like a lock side puts a considerable strain on its lanyard and its attachment to the boat. Check all cleats or eyes intended for fenders. Screw holes may have to be plugged to give the screws a grip. If the inside is accessible, bolts through may be better. If experience has shown that the hanging fenders are not in the best places, now may be the time to reposition them.

As with wood rubbing strips thickness is valuable in a hanging fender,

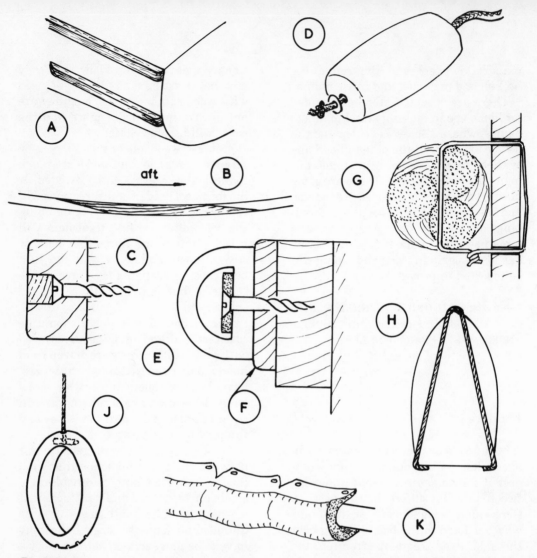

Fig. 21

but appearance requires them to be of only moderate size. Most modern fenders are moulded rubber or plastic. If the lanyard goes through, see that the knot below is large enough and there is a washer to prevent the knot pulling through (D). If the lanyard is attached to a tab with a hole at the top of the fender, this is the part that fails first. There is not much that can be done if this breaks, although with some materials it is possible to cut the tab off and pull the lanyard through the fender. The lanyard is better spliced than knotted to the tab.

Rope fenders were once popular and they have a traditional appearance. However, they collect grit and will absorb water if they are made of natural fibre. There is probably still nothing to equal rope for a situation such as the bow of a canal boat. Rope fenders should be frequently hosed to remove grit and they should be hung to dry whenever possible. A canvas band sewn around a hanging rope fender looks smart and does something to prevent embedded grit doing damage. A plastic-coated fabric is cleaner than ordinary canvas.

There may be permanent fendering around a boat instead of hanging fenders. This needs to be more substantial than it often is. Hollow rubber fendering needs a strip of metal or wood to prevent it sagging (E). Screws are sprung through holes in the outer rubber. Such fendering can be held off and therefore made more effective by a strip of wood against the normal wood rubbing strip (F).

A traditional all-round fender is stout rope. New rope is expensive, but a thick piece of old rope may be given a useful new life in this way. Sagging rope looks bad so it should be tensioned as it is fitted. One good way of fitting is to use copper wire through the rope and close-fitting holes in the hull (G). To get the rope tight, bend it around the stem and pull it straight back to the corners

of the transom, where it is fixed (H). The ends are securely whipped first. If a good tension is got on the rope in this way and it is then pulled out to the gunwales and fixed at intervals, there should be no difficulty with later sagging.

Some of the best fenders are old tyres, but they cannot be disguised and for this reason are rarely used. However, a few tyre fenders may be worth carrying to use in particularly rough and dirty locks or against commercial wharfs. A hole may be cut or drilled through one side, then a rope taken through and knotted to a piece of wood. Make some drain holes at the other side, otherwise it is very difficult to get rid of the last of any trapped water (J). A small tyre, no more than motor scooter size, may be given a canvas cover. Two circles of canvas are sewn inside-out by machine or hand slightly more than halfway around, then turned the right way and the tyre inserted and the rest of the stitching done by hand. The result is an acceptable-looking fender.

Tyres may be cut and fixed along the edge of a dock or landing stage (K). A knife will cut a rubber tyre if it is lubricated with water, but a hacksaw, also lubricated with water, is better, particularly as it will have to go through steel wire in some tyres. If the sides of the tyre are cut into at intervals so the tyre can be straightened out with the tread in a continuous length, one tyre can make quite a long piece of stage fendering. If the home mooring is alongside a stage, tyre fendering obviates the need for hanging fenders, so their life is prolonged.

Ferro-cement hulls

Marine paint makers have special primers for ferro-cement, that should be used as specified before finishing with normal yacht paints. New or repaired ferro-cement should be left at least a month before painting.

The method of repair depends on the extent of the damage. Cement and sand mixture can be used to fill small damage. If the hull has been distorted due to impact, the damage may be jacked out from inside, then cracked and broken cement picked out and new material worked in. There must be none of the reinforcing wire or other metal breaking the surface. Exposed wire ends that cannot be buried should be drilled into and the hole plugged with cement or epoxy glue. If additional netting has to be used in a repair, this should be buried as deep as the original wire.

Fiddles

A boat is an unstable platform for domestic activities and if it is used on tidal water things that are normally

level may tilt considerably. Hence the use of fiddles to keep pots on cookers and prevent crockery sliding off tables. If the fiddles are insecure and liable to come away they may be more dangerous than if they were not there, as they may be trusted to hold, say, boiling water and an accident could ensue.

Any fiddles should be tested for security, by putting on at least as much load as they may be expected to hold. If there are any screw fixings or adjustments, separate them and check threads. If there are lugs fitting in brackets, see that any screw fastenings are secure.

Clean thoroughly. Food stains or particles of food should be removed. A metal fiddle will benefit from polishing. A wooden fiddle should be painted or varnished. Do not leave bare wood that will absorb liquids. If the wood fiddle will be near hot containers, use polyurethane or other heat-resistant finish.

Filters, fuel

It is important that fuel reaching the engine is clean and it is important that it gets there in sufficient quantity. A filter that does its job in stopping impurities may get so clogged that sufficient fuel does not get through. How frequently a filter should be inspected and cleaned depends on many factors and it is better to inspect too often than not enough. A boat normally used in placid waters and then taken on the sea may shake up sediment in the tank enough to block a filter.

If the filter is the usual wire gauze, wash it in clean petrol. Wash out dirt by pouring through the opposite way to normal flow. If possible, avoid poking with anything, as this may enlarge holes. If there are signs of water in the filter, run some fuel to waste from the tank to swill out water in the pipe. Water is often present and a small quantity in the tank should not matter.

It is unwise to leave petrol unused in a tank for long periods. If the boat is expected to be left unused for several months, drain off petrol and use it elsewhere.

Make sure all filters are checked, including any in fillers. An inboard installation may have a filter under the tank and another near the carburettor.

see also FUEL SYSTEM.

Filters, water

If engine cooling is by water drawn through the hull and expelled after use, there should be a coarse strainer at the inlet and a filter of large area inside the boat. The outside strainer can only be inspected when the boat dries out or is hauled out, but any blockage should be poked out – not pushed inwards. At the same time, check security of fastenings of the strainer and skin fitting.

There should be a sea cock inside the skin fitting and immediately before the filter. Check this for leakage – adjust and tighten if necessary. Glands may need repacking. String soaked in graphite grease may be used if no other packing material is available.

The filter should be of large area. Even then, in some waters, there may be so much dirt that inspection and cleaning will be needed every time the motor is used. Withdraw the filter and wash it – preferably using water under pressure from a hose. When the boat is hauled out, use the hose to blow through from inside before replacing the filter parts.

It is unusual for there to be a filter in a drinking water system, but they are sometimes used. Many taps and water outlets, such as showers, include a filter. A tap may have a sand trap screwed inside its outlet. This can be felt inside the end and usually unscrewed by hand. Cork or rubber pressed against it will give a grip. A shower head may be contaminated by lime as well as impurities, due to hot water. If it is dismantled, this may be washed clean, but a scrubbing brush may be needed for caked lime.

The filler pipe of a drinking water system may contain a filter. Check and clean this, and see that the cap fits properly. Stiff threads may be eased with candle wax.

materials, not on fuel or electrical fires.

Fire risks are minimized with good ventilation.

see also BOTTLED GAS; VENTILATION.

Firefighting equipment

Most small craft are equipped with dry powder fire extinguishers for hand use. There is no direct servicing that should be done by the owner, but there will be a limit to the life of the contents and after the expiry date the extinguisher should be recharged by the makers. Check the mountings, which are not always of damp-resisting construction, and see that they are sound but will release the extinguisher when required. Some painting or oiling may be necessary.

Check that the extinguishers are located satisfactorily. As far as possible they should be within reach from outside as well as inside a cabin. One should be near the engine and another near the galley. Whether there are others depends on the size of the craft. For galley use there may also be fire blankets for smothering fires.

Larger craft may have automatic or remotely controlled extinguishers. These ought to be the subject of a regular maintenance contract with the makers.

A bag of sand will smother burning spilled fuel. Buckets on board should have lanyards so they can collect water from overside for firefighting, but only use water on burning wood or other

First aid kit

As medical help will not always be close at hand, a first aid kit must be regarded as an essential item of equipment. The scope of its contents will depend on where the boat is being taken and how far it will be from medical aid. If an accident occurs on a canal cruiser, the first aid treatment will be only what is needed until a doctor can be reached, which may not be long. On an ocean voyage, the kit may have to be used for treatment that would normally only be undertaken by a doctor. Maintenance of the first aid kit must take account of the intended use of the boat.

The first aid kit should be part of the boat's permanent equipment, rather than something that is taken home, and possibly forgotten. It should have its own stowage and everyone on board should know where that is. It should include some instructional material, in case it is the expert who has the accident. Ideally this should be a manual of a first aid organization.

Most calls on the first aid outfit are likely to be for dealing with minor cuts, so include plenty of adhesive dressings, plus some lint and bandages and a pair of scissors which are not allowed to be taken from the kit for other uses. Burns and scalds need quick treatment, so see that suitable materials are included. For headaches there should be aspirin or an alternative and even for short sea voyages there should be seasickness remedies. How much more is included depends on the extent of the voyage.

It should be the rule that if anything is used from the first aid kit, a replacement is made soon. Check that this has been done. If the kit is old, compare its contents with a modern book of instructions. With increased knowledge and modern materials, some of the older things have been superseded.

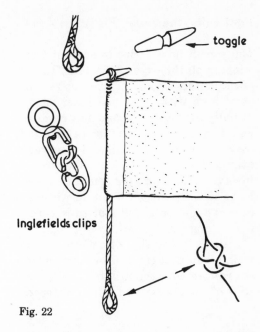

toggle

Inglefields clips

Fig. 22

Flags (Fig. 22)

Any flag used afloat should be hoisted with a halyard and fitted with a rope to allow for this. The rope extends below the flag a distance equal to the depth of the flag. Any method of attachment should allow for the flag being hoisted as close up as possible. It is considered incorrect to have any appreciable space above the flag. A wooden or plastic toggle may be spliced into the rope and this drawn well into the flag, then sewn through the splice. An eye at the end of the flag rope engages with a toggle in the halyard or is joined to it with a sheet bend.

Inglefield's clips can be used instead of toggles. They give a quick means of attaching and removing, but make sure they are arranged to come close at the top.

A flag will soon fray more once it has begun to break up, so sew over any ragged edges. Cutting down to get a new clean edge is not acceptable. A flag must retain its proper proportion and shape. Damage in the body of the flag may be darned, but if a patch is required, this should be matching bunting. If smartness is to be retained, a replacement may be required.

Foot rails (toe rails) (Fig. 23)

Many craft have strips to prevent feet slipping off the edge of the deck. To be effective they should be at least 2½ cm (1 in) high with a vertical inner edge. Usually they are wood and may cover a joint in wooden construction (A). Water may get below a foot rail and start rot, even in itself if there is no other wood involved. This can be a source of deck leaks and the onset of rot in wooden construction, so check foot rails carefully along their length.

If there is any sign of moisture or a visible gap that could let water under the rail, remove the rail and check the state of what is exposed. Allow water to

dry out. Methylated spirits will speed drying. If actual gaps are uncovered, they must be filled. A mixture of glue and sawdust can be used. A flexible stopping may be pressed in. Resin and glassfibre strands may be used in gaps in wood or glassfibre construction. Bed the rail in similar materials and screw down tightly. Any new screws should be counterbored and plugged (B).

There may be an additional problem at gaps in the foot rail where space is allowed for water to run off or fender ropes to pass. The deck sealing at these points may have suffered. Make sure deck canvas or plastic is still sound at these places. If there is no covering, there should be a good coating of paint, preferably with one of the thicker mastics as used on decks. The gaps may be a source of deck leaks more than loose foot rails. When the foot rails are removed a deck with no special treatment may have glass or fabric cloth let into the space and a short distance under the rail (C), but avoid having a ridge that will interfere with water running away.

see also DECKS; PAINT.

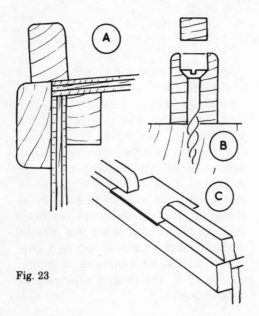

Fig. 23

Frames and timbers (Fig. 24)

Transverse strength in a wooden boat is provided by frames which are built-up or by those that are sprung to the shape of the hull, and may be called timbers. As frames often go into a hull early in

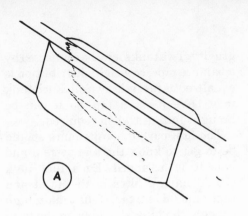

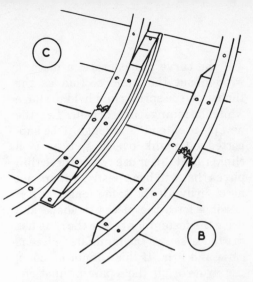

Fig. 24

construction, it is usually difficult or impossible to remove them for replacement. If a repair is needed, patching rather than replacement is normally preferable.

A cracked frame member should be checked for distortion and wedged or propped back into shape while a patch is put on one or both sides, with glue and fastenings taken through (A). If the damage is at an angle, it may be possible to prise off a plywood gusset and replace it, but make sure the frame is back as near to its original shape as possible before the new piece is fixed. With extensive damage to a frame repair pieces should be long enough to transfer loads from one joint to another, possibly with a patching piece of at least as large a section as the part it is repairing.

Bent frames or timbers are more common in small boats and cracking is most likely in a clinker hull, because it flexes. A very occasional broken timber may not matter, but when there are several close together, they should be repaired. In some parts of a boat it may be possible to remove a broken timber and fit another. Fastenings should be drilled and punched out, but try to avoid enlarging holes in the hull. A flexible wood has to be used, not only for ease in fitting, but to allow for flexing of the hull in use. Ash is commonly used, but this is not very durable and should be well protected with varnish or paint.

A new frame may be jammed to a preliminary curve some time before fitting, then finally sprung to shape. For a tight curve, soak it in hot water. Prop it into place or have a helper hold it, while fastenings are entered, working from the keel outwards. For a simple single break anywhere and where getting a timber out and replacing it would be difficult, it is simpler to double up alongside the damage.

69

If the curve is moderate, a piece of wood about the same section as the timber can be sprung and held to shape while fastenings are driven. Let the new piece extend far enough to be supported on plank overlaps, if it is a clinker boat (B), or use two or three thin pieces that will bend easily, but are not necessarily all the same length (C). If possible force the pieces to shape and drive the fastenings before the glue has started to set, so the laminated piece is close and firm. If this cannot be done, use struts to jam the repair laminations in place until the glue has set. The assembly can then be taken out and cleaned up before it is fixed.

Such a laminated doubling-up piece may lack the flexibility of solid wood, but for the short length it occupies, this should not matter.

see also ADHESIVES; FASTENINGS; LAMINATING.

Fuel system

Petrol or other fuel is carried in a single tank for a small boat inboard engine. If much fuel is to be carried, it may be divided between several tanks. In the simplest system the single tank is high enough to feed the engine by gravity. If there are more tanks and they are low, there may be a pump, which may feed the engine direct or pump fuel to a header tank, which feeds the engine by gravity. Two tanks may be connected by a balance pipe, so weight distribution is equalized as fuel is drawn off. Each tank may have its own tap, so it can be brought into use when required.

The first part of maintenance should be to get to know the fuel system and how it is arranged. Each fuel tank should have a filter in its outlet and there should be a tap. If the tank is high enough, the filter should be in the form of a sump, which can be taken out and emptied. Besides dirt there may be water accumulated in the tank. This may be due as much to condensation as to any carelessness or leakage at the filler pipe. Normal boat motions can shake up sediment and water. Clean the filter. Be careful not to let any petrol escape into the bilges. A small amount of petrol can join with air to form an explosive mixture.

There may be another filter near the carburettor, either as a separate unit or combined with the coupling to the carburettor. Do not overlook its presence if it is in the coupling. This is the second line of defence, if anything gets through the tank filter. Despite the filters foreign matter may get through to the carburettor and a very tiny particle of dirt may be enough to interfere with the proper functioning of some carburettors.

If an engine is functioning properly, it is probably best to leave the carburettor alone. The bowl may be removed and the correct behaviour of the float checked. If there is any sediment in the bowl, wash the bowl and float with petrol, which is then thrown away. So far as possible, avoid handling the float or the inside of the bowl after cleaning.

If the carburettor is a type with fixed jets in nipples that screw in and a jet becomes blocked, treat the part very carefully when unscrewing and replacing. If possible, blow through the jet with a compressed air line, rather than by mouth, as moisture from the breath getting in the tiny hole may cause more trouble.

Observe the action of throttle and choke. It is very unlikely that any adjustment will be needed, but see that fixing screws are tight and see whether linkage to remote controls may need lubricating.

Unions and taps in the fuel system should need little attention. The usual union may be checked for tightness and screwed a little tighter, but it is unwise to dismantle a union just to look at it, as some types are not intended to be reused, and a complete new union or a new inside would be needed.

The fuel system for an outboard motor with an integral tank is a very compressed version of that used for an inboard motor installation, but filter cleaning and security of unions is just as important. If an outboard motor has a remote tank, this should be drained and cleaned, rather than leave it for long periods partly filled. The flexible pipe to the motor is liable to wear, so check it occasionally for damage. See that the end unions are secure and the attachment to the motor closes properly. Any air leaks along the way will affect engine performance and any leaks of fuel are potentially dangerous.

Except for the flexible pipe for a remote tank connected to an outboard motor, there should usually be no flexible pipes in a fuel system. If it is unavoidable for any reason, make sure the pipe is as short as possible and of a synthetic rubber that is immune to attack by petrol. See that the end fittings are secure and positive. Do not depend on a push-on arrangement.

If fuel is carried in cans, they should be metal and designed for the purpose. Petrol will attack many plastics. If the can is intended for transferring fuel to a tank while afloat, use a type with a good spout. To avoid the risk of a spark due to static electricity, link the can to the metal of the tank before pouring. So far as possible avoid the use of loose cans of fuel. Anything that leaks into the bilges is difficult to remove and quite a small amount of petrol leaking may result in vapour being trapped where it can form an explosive mixture with air. Pumping out the bilges will not always remove the hazard.

see also ENGINE ELECTRICAL SYSTEM; FILTERS, FUEL; INBOARD ENGINES, DIESEL; INBOARD ENGINES, PETROL; INBOARD PETROL ENGINE FAULTS; REMOTE CONTROLS.

Generator

If the boat engine drives a generator via a belt, check that the belt is tight enough to drive without slip. If it is an alternator, it is unwise for an unskilled owner to try any other maintenance.

If the generator is a dynamo, suspected of inefficiency, disconnect the wires from the end opposite the drive. Have the engine ticking over while a test bulb with leads is used to check output. Connect one wire across both of the dynamo terminals and earth the other lead to the engine. The bulb should glow and slight acceleration should brighten it, but avoid much acceleration which will blow the bulb. If there is no light, the dynamo should be removed and inspected.

If loose solder or other displaced material can be seen through the end plate, the dynamo is beyond repair and should be replaced. Otherwise, remove the screws holding the end plate and withdraw it. This allows the armature assembly to be withdrawn. At the end of this is the commutator, which should be wiped with a cloth moistened with petrol and the grooves between the segments should be gently cleaned out with a needle or pin. If the commutator shows much wear, this part or the complete dynamo must be exchanged.

New brushes may be needed. Deal with one at a time. Unscrew the terminal tag and pull the wire and brush clear of the guide. Before putting in the new brush and wire, clean the guide by brushing and wiping with a cloth moistened with petrol. Check that the spring is in good order. With both new brushes fitted, the dynamo can be reassembled, but so the brushes will clear the commutator during assembly, hook the spring ends back until completion, then release them with a fine screwdriver through the holes in the end plate.

Glassfibre (Fig. 25)

This is a material which has not yet found a universal name. Glass reinforced plastic (g.r.p.) is a better description, but it may also be called Fibreglass, which is actually the trade name of the reinforcing material. Most boat owners are familiar with the finished product as this is the most usual material for boat hulls today.

Nearly all glassfibre boats are made of polyester resin in which is embedded several layers of glass material in the form of very fine filaments, which can be made up into woven cloth or may be in random pieces called chopped strand mat. Some of this may be visible through the resin. The natural colour is off-white, but pigments can be used in the resin during manufacture.

A boat hull, or other part, is made in a mould, usually with the outside towards the mould and this surface reproduces the finish of the mould in a gel coat. Although the gel coat may start with a flawless high gloss, the resin is not very hard and some of the first maintenance with a glassfibre hull is concerned with restoring the finish.

Soap or synthetic detergent can be used to remove dirt from glassfibre. There are polishes available for use on glassfibre, but a car polish can be used. A damp cloth and pumice powder or household scouring powder can be used on a worn patch, then metal polish used before the final polish to restore a surface.

The gel coat is not very thick and normal use will soon wear through it. If damage or scoring is deep enough to expose the glassfibre threads there is risk of water absorption. Capillary action causes water to flow into the area around the damage. A small amount of absorption is not serious and may be inevitable underwater. Difficulty comes with freezing conditions when the absorbed water may freeze and expand, causing a wrinkled or puckered surface.

Scratches and other damage that admit water can be filled with resin, either bought with the necessary accelerator or as a plastic putty. Repair kits sold by motor sundries firms are a good source of small quantities of basic repair materials. It is important to follow the maker's instructions concerning proportions and temperatures. The usual mixture will not set in outdoor winter temperatures. An alternative to polyester resin is epoxy (Araldite). This is a two-part substance, mixed just before use. For filling small cracks, it has a better adhesion than polyester, but because of its cost it is not the usual choice for larger repairs.

When a glassfibre hull comes from its mould, it has a wax release agent still adhering to it. Sometimes this lasts for a long time and would interfere with the adhesion of new resin. Some polishes might also affect it. Wipe around any damage with a cloth soaked in a solvent, such as paint thinner or methylated spirit.

Scrape out a crack and fill it with resin sufficient to stand a little above the surface. When this has set, use fine abrasive paper to level the outside, then use pumice powder followed by polishes to restore the surface.

If the trouble is a crack that goes quite deep, it may be better to scrape out fully, possibly right through. In this case, sand around the inside of the damage and use a patch of glass cloth or chopped strand mat bedded in resin. Apply the resin with a brush using a stippling up-and-down action. Sanding just before fixing any patch is important, to get the best adhesion. If the sides of the damage can be undercut (A) security of the repair will be increased. Pull out some strands of glass from mat and have this ready. Push resin into the crack after any backing patch has 'gelled' (this is the initial partial setting which takes place in ten minutes or so, according to temperature). Press glass strands into this, but make sure none project above the surface. When the repair has set, clean off the outside.

If the damage is such that filling cracks would not be adequate, cut away the damage to an even shape. This can be done by drilling and using a hacksaw blade or other fine saw. Rounded corners are better than angular ones (B). There is no need for a symmetrical shape. File the edges, preferably to a double bevel (C).

If the boat can be tilted, work from the inside and have the damage downwards

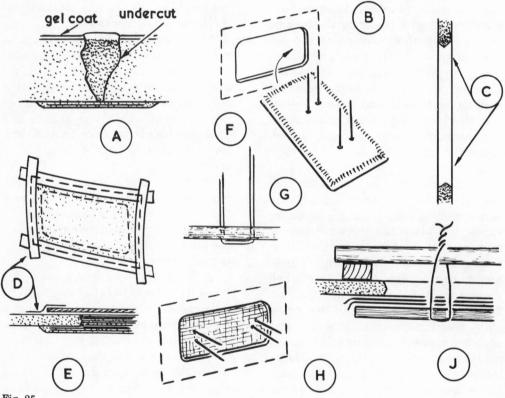

Fig. 25

so gravity will help the flow of resin into the hole. Sand an inch or so around the inside of the hole just before making the repair. If the boat cannot be tilted, it is possible to get thixotropic resin which resists running on a near-vertical surface.

Have a piece of card on the outside. Coat its inner surface with release agent or use a smooth piece of plastic. Fix this with adhesive tape (D).

Mix enough resin to form a gel coat. Brush this inside the hole on to the outside pieces, making sure it goes well up to the edges of the hole. Let this gel, then follow with more layers of resin and glassfibre. Use the brush with a stippling action and work on each layer until the appearance shows that the resin has impregnated the mat. When sufficient thickness has been built up fix one or two further layers of mat to overlap the damage inside (E). This need not be done in a continuous process, but do not leave one layer to fully harden before following with another. When the whole repair has hardened or cured, remove the card, then sand and polish the outside.

There are parts of some hulls where it is impossible to work from the inside, so all of a repair has to be done from the outside. This involves more work to get a satisfactory finish, so working from inside should be arranged whenever possible. To make a repair solely from outside, the damage has to be trimmed so a backing piece can be passed through the hole and turned in line. This means cutting the hole so it is larger one way than the other (F).

Make a backing piece of card or hardboard that is large enough to overlap the hole by about 1 in. It may not be recovered later and will be left inside, possibly to drop into the bilges. Card might become pulpy and clog a bilge pump, but card is better than hardboard if there is much curve to the hull. Sand around the inside of the hole for the amount of overlap, by reaching through with abrasive paper.

Run one or two pieces of copper wire through the backing piece with their ends standing up. Cut two pieces of glassfibre cloth or mat slightly larger than the backing piece. Put them on it, with plenty of resin, leaving the wire ends projecting (G). Put more resin around the inside of the hole. Pass the assembly through the hole and turn it into position, using the wires to handle it and pull it into position (H). Use one or two strips of wood on blocks outside. Twist the wire ends together over these to pull the patch tight inside (J).

Leave all of this long enough to completely cure. Cut off the wire ends close to the glassfibre. Fill the hole with more layers of glassfibre and resin. Make sure the outer layer is resin only and allow for sanding this down and polishing.

Although it is possible to use pigment in repair resin it is almost impossible to get a true match of colour. After a hull has reached the stage where much of the original gloss has gone and repairs have had to be made, it is better to paint it all over.

Paint manufacturers have their own recommendations for painting glassfibre. Some require a special primer, but the usual finish is polyurethane. Many of the other marine paints do not have a satisfactory adhesion to glassfibre. In any case, it is important to prepare the surface. Dirt and grease must be removed and there must be no sign of release agent or polish. Any remaining gloss should be removed by scouring with pumice powder or other fine abrasive. Once the preparations have been made and the right paint system selected, the actual application is straightforward as a glassfibre surface is usually smoother than most other materials.

Polyester and epoxy resin will bond to other materials, so it is possible to make a glassfibre repair to boats made of wood or metal. This can be resin and glassfibre as used in construction or one of the prepared mixtures or kits sold by car sundries firms. The bond has to be to the bare material. Paint, varnish, surface grease and dirt should all be removed and the surface roughened. Damaged wood need not be trimmed, except as necessary for neatness. If edges are cut, a roughly sawn edge is better than a carefully planed or chiselled one. Allow for overlapping with glassfibre and resin inside and clean the inner surface down to bare wood. Roughen the inner surface. Scraping with a saw drawn sideways in several directions will produce a suitable surface.

Although polyester has been used for metal repairs, it is better to use epoxy. Coarsely filed edges and inner surfaces roughened with coarse abrasive will be adequate preparation. Jagged edges may be left, providing they do not project where they would disfigure. Be particularly careful to remove grease and have the surface dry.

With the damage prepared, a repair is carried out in the same way as on a glassfibre hull. As the outside will not have to be polished, it does not matter if there is roughness to sand down later. Allow for a good overlap inside the damage, which may be built up to give strength if the hull is thin metal. Sand the outside level after the repair has cured, then paint over to match the surrounding surface, but use the paint maker's recommended primer and choose polyurethane, if possible.

see also ALUMINIUM; BUOYANCY, RESERVE; CARVEL PLANKING; PLYWOOD REPAIRS; STEEL HULLS.

Grab rails (Fig. 26)

Hand holds are important on any small cabin craft. They must have holes large enough for a hand to pass through and

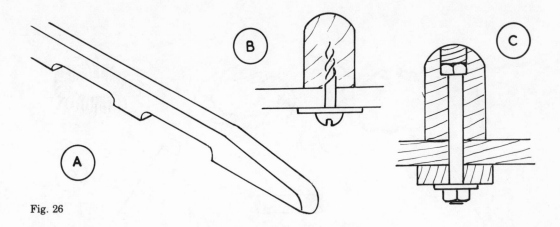

Fig. 26

grip (A). Check smoothness inside the holes. See that any rail will take the full weight of an adult. Check the security of fastenings. There may be wood screws from inside additional to glue or resin under the rail outside. If they have pulled in, use new screws with large washers (B).

A stronger attachment is made with bolts through and if the cabin top or other part is thin, it is better to have a strip of wood inside for the length of the rail (C). If there is any internal structure that the rail passes over, such as bulkheads or beams, long screws from outside into these will add strength.

Wooden grab rails may serve a decorative purpose over an otherwise bare expanse. It is worthwhile to keep them in a good varnished state if they are made of an attractive hardwood, so sanding and revarnishing should be normal maintenance.

Grommets (Fig. 27)

This is the name given to a sewn reinforced hole in canvas, although it is sometimes used to mean an eyelet. The edge may be strengthened with a metal ring or by a rope or cord ring, which may be separately called a grommet. To make this, cut a piece of three-strand rope of suitable size about four times the diameter hole required. Take out one strand without disturbing its lay. Twist this together, letting the parts fit into each other (A), until you have been around three times to make a continuous rope ring. Cut off the ends (B).

Cut a cross in the canvas and put the metal or rope ring over it. Have a needle and doubled thread ready. Sew over the ring, letting the canvas turn up inside it. Let the stitches be close enough to touch inside the ring. Vary the lengths of adjoining stitches so as to spread the

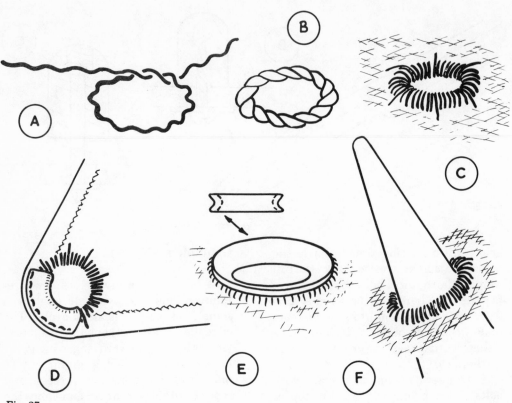

Fig. 27

strain on the canvas (C). The stitches of an old grommet may have chafed. Putting more stitches over them, but going through different places in the canvas, will usually make a good repair. Damage after that can be avoided if a piece of soft leather is threaded through the hole and wrapped over where the load comes, then a few stitches are put through it and the canvas (D). Wetting the leather allows it to be moulded to shape.

A grommet over a rope ring sometimes has a round liner or thimble enclosed (E). This is sprung in and care is needed to get the tension right on the grommet as it is made to allow for this. Have the liner ready, then force the grommet open over a fid or other spike (F). As soon as it is taken off, spring the liner in before it has had time to go back to size.

see also CANVAS REPAIRS; EYELETS.

78

Guardrails

Pulpit, pushpit, guardrails and their stanchions, plus lifelines, make safety devices that are important items to be checked as users assume they are in good condition and failure could have serious consequences.

Wood screws to a deck are inadvisable. If there have to be any, the same base should also have through fastenings. If all holes in the base come over solid parts that will not allow a fastening through, it may be advisable to extend the base.

The security of wires forming guardrails depends on their end fittings. Check splices, swaged ends or screwed fittings. Examine tensioning devices for distortion or wear. Apply the loads that might be expected in emergency and see the effect. Wires may need retensioning. Where parts of the wires take down to give access, see that pelican hooks or other fastenings function properly, have sound pins and hooks and that their attachments are secure.

Halyards (Fig. 28)

Most sail halyards have one part under strain and a long tail which is only loaded briefly during hoisting. It helps to get the most from the rope to turn a halyard end-for-end occasionally.

If a halyard passes through a hollow mast, a new length of rope can be drawn through by sewing its end to the old one (A).

If a halyard has to be passed through a hollow mast without the help of an old one, a light line should be dropped through first, using a piece of scrap lead as a 'mouse' (B). It can bend around the masthead sheave and its weight will take the line down the mast. At the lower outlet a bent wire will get it out

(C). If there is enough clearance to allow it to pass, the cord can be joined to the new halyard with a variation on the sheet bend, that turns both ends back (D). If there is not much clearance it will be better to overlap the ends and either tightly whip or sew through (E).

see also MASTS; SPARS.

Heaters

A cabin heater should be fixed. If gas, its connections should be via screwed joints and metal pipes. Flexible hose, as sometimes used in caravans, is not used on a boat. If paraffin, it should be a type

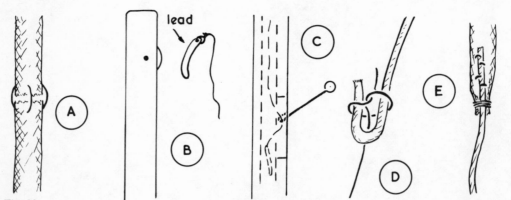

Fig. 28

intended for use afloat. A domestic paraffin heater may be unsafe in a cabin and most are made of materials that would soon suffer in damp conditions.

Any flame heater burns oxygen from the air and exhausts dangerous fumes. There should be a flue or other escape for the products of combustion. One maintenance job is checking that this is functioning properly. In some heaters air for burning is drawn from outside via a duct. This should also be checked. Some of these heaters have the flame sealed from using cabin air and warmth comes from a heat exchanger. This type of heater requires no servicing, other than seeing that inlet and outlet points are clear.

If the flame burns air from the cabin, see that good ventilation is maintained and that it cannot be sealed accidentally or deliberately.

In a larger craft where heated air is circulated as a form of central heating, the maker's handbook should be consulted about maintenance requirements, but if it is functioning correctly, it may be left alone, except for cleaning the gas jets.

see also BOTTLED GAS; VENTILATION.

Hinges (Fig. 29)

There is a very large variety of hinges manufactured, but only a compara-

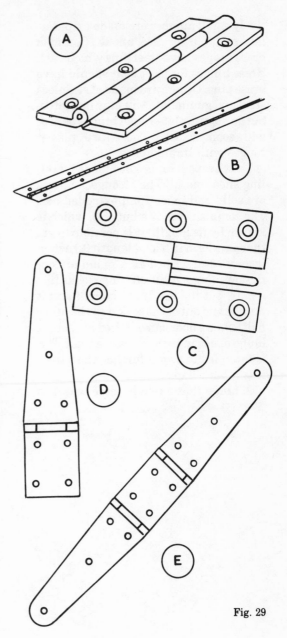

Fig. 29

81

tively small number are made in materials suitable for use afloat. Common brass hinges have steel pins which rust. Brass hinges for use afloat should have brass pins. Others are made of stainless steel and gunmetal. Any may be plated, but do not use plated steel hinges as rust will soon attack. There are plastic hinges with limited uses.

The cheapest hinges are made by rolling sheet metal. The strongest hinges are solid and made from extruded bar. The common type is a butt (A), which is known by its length. It is possible to get the same form in a long length (B), when it may be described as a piano or continuous hinge. A lift-off hinge looks like a butt, but the pin is in one half and it may be slid out of the socket in the other half (C), so a door can be lifted off. A butt hinge opens to little more than flat. If it is intended to swing further than that, it is a back-flap.

A hinge that extends some way is a strap hinge and is single tail if the long part is one way (D) or double tail if it is long both ways. A variation is a skylight hinge (E), with a centre portion.

Horns

Horns are the usual means of indicating a change of course, acting as fog warnings or attracting the attention of a lock keeper. Aerosol types are popular, but check that there are spare canisters. It is also advisable to have a second horn, operated by hand or mouth. If the main horn is electrical, check its working and adjust it for the best note. Deal with any corrosion of terminals. Check the security of its mounting. An alternative type of horn should be carried, in case of battery failure. If this is a portable type it should have its own stowage place.

Ignition system

Electricity for ignition in nearly all inboard petrol engines comes from a battery. It goes through a switch to a coil, which builds up the low voltage to the high voltage needed, and this is connected to a distributor which directs electricity to each spark plug as needed. The alternative to this system is a magneto, which is a generator driven by the engine it is serving. As the magneto does not generate electricity until it is turning, the engine has to be turned over by a handle or electric motor – or a cord in the case of an outboard motor. Some older inboard motors had both systems, so the engine was started on battery and coil, then changed over to magneto when the engine was running fast enough to make the magneto produce a good enough spark.

The coil needs no servicing except to see that the cover is clean and dry, and the leads are secure – particularly the heavy central cable connection carrying the high tension cable to the distributor.

The distributor is mechanically driven from the engine. The rotating shaft drives a cam working a make-and-break system of spring-loaded contacts. The number of times they open and close depends on the number of cylinders. Also on this shaft is a rotor arm which directs electricity to the same number of terminals as there are cylinders.

The distributor cap carries a central lead from the coil and other leads to the spark plugs. Check externally for cleanliness and tightness of the cable connections. Inside the cap check that the central carbon brush, if fitted, moves easily.

In most distributors the rotor arm will lift off, without the need to release any locking arrangement. Lubrication is necessary, but must be sparing. A few drops of oil can be dropped in the space alongside the cam. The cam faces may be lubricated by an oily finger. If there is a central cam exposed when the rotor arm is removed, put a little oil on this.

Any fault in the distributor is likely to be at the contact breaker points. These open and close in relation to each other and the sparking between them causes pitting. The simplest and best treatment for pitted points is to replace with a new contact set. In an emergency the pitted surfaces can be filed to present new flatter surfaces. In both cases the gap has to be set.

To set filed or new points, a feeler gauge is needed. The handbook specifies the amount of maximum gap. With the distributor open and the rotor arm removed, turn the engine slowly by hand until the cam has opened the gap to the maximum. Loosen the securing screw and move the contact breaker baseplate with a screwdriver until the points just touch the feeler gauge. Retighten the screw and check the gap again. For the distributor of a four-stroke inboard engine it is advisable to carry a contact set as spare. If the engine is one of the same family as a car engine, the distributor will be the same and the parts easily obtained from a car sundries firm.

see also BATTERY; ENGINE ELECTRICAL SYSTEM; INBOARD ENGINES, PETROL; INBOARD PETROL ENGINE FAULTS.

Inboard engines, diesel

As there is no electric ignition system in a diesel engine, one of the commonest causes of trouble in a boat engine is avoided. The most important aspect of diesel engine servicing concerns the maintenance of fuel quality and quantity. There should be adequate filters in the fuel supply so any scale, dirt or water from the tank cannot get down the line. A filter at the filler is also advisable, particularly if filling has to be from cans and not direct from a pump nozzle. Inspect and clean filters – if this seems to be too frequent judging by the lack of foreign matter found, this is better than leaving them too long. If any fuel is recovered after draining, filter it before returning it to the tank. This can be done through non-fluffy cloth, such as nylon or silk.

Water cooling of a diesel engine is similar to that of a petrol engine. Although there is no electrical ignition system, the engine may have electric starting and drive a generator, so these parts should receive the same maintenance as described for a petrol engine. A diesel engine requires very little routine maintenance. Any attention to the injectors or their pump should be left to an expert. The outside of the engine should be kept clean. Any leaking or spilling of fuel should be corrected to avoid unpleasant smells.

Diesel engines are heavier than petrol engines and more prone to vibration, so there may be flexible mountings that should be inspected for wear and deterioration. Whether they can be replaced by the owner or not depends on their type and the engine size, but if one mounting has deteriorated it is probable that it would be advisable to replace them all, and this will probably mean lifting tackle and expert help.

see also FUEL SYSTEM; INBOARD ENGINES, PETROL.

Inboard engines, petrol

The majority of inboard motors have many points in common with car engines and some of them are from the same basic power units. An owner with experience of doing routine servicing to a car engine will find that the work on a marine engine is very similar. A marine engine does not get anything like the amount of use that a car engine does, but servicing should come at shorter intervals. The engine is mounted low in a boat, so may be more difficult to get at. The fact that it stands for long periods in what is usually a damp atmosphere, may mean a different sort of deterioration. If a car engine breaks down, it may be a nuisance, but is not often a danger, and outside help can usually be found quickly. If a boat engine breaks down, the crew and their boat may be in a dangerous situation and outside assistance may not be obtainable. This means that anyone going afloat with an inboard engine, particularly offshore, should have a reasonable basic knowledge of how to deal with the motor, even if ashore anything under the car bonnet is left to the man from the garage.

This section deals with general maintenance. Particular items are dealt with separately – see end of this section.

Most inboard motors are four-stroke, although a few are two-stroke. The maintenance of two-stroke motors is similar in many ways to outboard motors. A four-stroke engine has valve gear. Fortunately, this requires only rare attention, but each cylinder has inlet and exhaust valves and loss of power or erratic running may be due to leaking valves. A keen amateur may grind and reset valves with the aid of the handbook, but any owner who doubts his ability should pass this work to an expert.

A motor needs fuel, mixed with air in the right proportion, a spark at each cylinder at the right time, a means of exhausting the spent gases and usually a water-cooling system. If the motor has been properly adjusted when installed, it is unlikely that trouble which develops will be due to the interior parts of the motor; it is more likely to be due to an auxiliary system.

As with a car engine, lubrication should be checked frequently. In most motors there is a dipstick. When oil has to be changed, it is difficult or impossible to drain via a screwed plug underneath, as in a car engine. There may be an oil pump installed, there may be a means of mounting one, or there may be an inspection panel to take off the side of the sump, where a pump can be inserted. There should be a tray or pan installed under the engine to prevent any waste oil going into the bilges. This tray may also have to be pumped out occasionally. It can be cleaned out with paraffin and wiped where it can be reached, in the interest of general cleanliness. If the state of the engine oil that is drawn out is such that the sump ought to be cleaned before refilling, this can be done with flushing oil, not paraffin.

If there is an oil filter, check with the handbook (or by examining the filter) on the frequency of changing or cleaning. The filter element may only have to be changed at alternate oil changes. Marine engines last a long time. Some older engines may have other oiling arrangements besides the sump. There may be points for the application of an oil can or grease gun or there may be screw-down greasers. There may be a drip feed lubricator. If there are any of these lubrication points, it is better to over-lubricate than under-lubricate. The amount that is wasted is negligible. The only exception may be if the lubrication is in the vicinity of electrical parts, when excess lubricant might affect electrical functioning.

If the motor is water-cooled, it may have an enclosed system with a heat-exchanger outside and usually beside the keel, with the same water circulating. This is similar to a car system, with the heat exchanger taking the place of the radiator. There will be a water pump to circulate the water. So long as the pump continues to work the only servicing will be topping up water and anti-freeze for cold weather, but this should rarely be necessary. Check if the pump has a lubrication point and deal with this occasionally.

Many motors are cooled by water drawn in by a pump through the bottom of the boat and ejected through the exhaust system, where the water aids in cooling the exhaust. Some water may be ejected via a pipe to a hole in the side of the boat, where the small stream of water serves to show that the cooling system is functioning. This should be checked when the engine is started and at intervals while it is running.

Such a system takes water as it comes, so mud and small pieces of solid debris may go through the system. The first item of protection is some sort of grill over the intake. It cannot be reached when the boat is afloat, although with some types of filter immediately inside, a limited amount of poking may be possible. Whenever the boat dries out or is hauled out, this grill should be inspected and any impurities cleared away.

There should be a seacock next to the hull. This should be bolted through the hull, possibly with the same bolts going through the grill outside. If any of this has to be dismantled, bed down on a new layer of jointing compound. The seacock will have a turning or screw-down action. Check that this closes properly and there is no drip.

There should be a filter above the seacock. How often this needs to be inspected depends on how dirty the water is, but if cooling water becomes restricted or the engine overheats, suspect a blockage in the filter. Some filters are tall enough to bring their top above the waterline. One of these can be opened and the filter element removed for cleaning without closing the seacock. Otherwise, the engine must be stopped and the seacock closed before opening the filter. The filter can be washed with water. The filter casing should be sealed tightly. This is on the suction side of the pump and poor sealing will result in the pump sucking air as well as water.

Correct functioning of the water pump can be checked by watching that a steady stream of water is ejected when the engine is running. Debris getting past the filter may obstruct the pump. A pump may be dismantled periodically if a fault is suspected, but water pumps usually give little trouble and are better left alone. The only other maintenance of the water system is to check that all joints are tight.

The exhaust system of a boat suffers from the corroding effect of exhaust gases in the same way as a car exhaust system and may also be attacked by salt, so the whole system may not have a very long life. Inspect for holes and disintegration due to corrosion. Stainless steel exhaust systems intended for cars may not be salt-water resistant, so check with the makers before using one as a replacement.

If any part of the exhaust system comes close to anything that would suffer if overheated or is in a place where it might be touched, wrapping with asbestos rope is a good protective treatment. In many boats the exhaust pipe goes out through the transom above the waterline. Check the security of the skin fitting and any bolts through it. Make sure the end of the exhaust pipe still makes a sound connection and has not corroded at the joint. It is usual to give the pipe a curve upwards not very far forward of the transom. Do not omit this in any replacement as this is to stop water, such as might come from an overtaking wave astern, getting back to the engine.

Although a marine engine does not have a car-type radiator and fan, there may be a similar belt driving a generator, water pump and other things. Failure of this belt might be serious. Check it and replace it when doubtful, before it actually breaks. Carry a spare. Excessive tensioning will shorten its life. Adjust so it is tight enough to drive without slipping, which will probably mean it can be flexed quite a bit from side to side on a wide gap between pulleys.

Parts of the electrical gear are dealt with under other headings, but in general check wiring for sound insulation. Old rubber insulation will become porous and absorb moisture so there are electrical leaks. More recent plastic insulation is less troublesome. Coat everything with a protective spray to keep out damp. Check end connections. Make sure all wires of a flexible cable make good contact with any attachments or fittings. Soldering is a secure way to make a joint. See that meeting surfaces are scraped clean and kept tight.

Cables should be no longer than necessary and if any replacements are made, let them be at least of the same gauge wire and thickness of insulation as the old cable. In the ignition system, in particular, thick short cables are necessary to carry the heavy current with the minimum loss on the way. Switches are as much a part of the system as the cables, so see that they have clean contacts and positive action. Any advantages of a good current-carrying system will be lost if there is one poor part along it where there is a restriction to current flow.

Examine the spark plugs. Hand cleaning is not really very effective. It is better to have them cleaned with the special equipment at a garage. Check the spark gap with a feeler gauge and set it if necessary by bending the outer contact. The exposed parts of a plug may suffer more than the parts inside the cylinder if the atmosphere is salty. Good plugs are vital to the smooth running of the engine and new ones should be fitted if you have any doubts about the old ones, but be careful to use only the types recommended by the makers. Use a protective spray on the plugs after their wires are connected.

It is good practice to keep a boat engine as clean as possible. Protect with paint, but use a heat-resistant paint on parts that get hot. Most aluminium paints will withstand heat. There may be no need to go as far as polishing copper pipes, but a clean engine encourages efficient handling and maintenance, and if any servicing has to be done, the work is less messy. Oil and grease can be wiped off with a cloth soaked in a solvent or degreasing fluid.

see also BATTERY; ENGINE ELECTRICAL SYSTEM; FUEL SYSTEM; IGNITION SYSTEM; INBOARD ENGINES, DIESEL; INBOARD PETROL ENGINE FAULTS; OUTBOARD MOTORS; REMOTE CONTROLS.

Inboard petrol engine faults

Problems with an inboard engine are mostly very similar to those that may be found with a car engine, so anyone with much experience of cars will not have much difficulty in diagnosing what has gone wrong if there is engine trouble.

Starting
If the battery starting does not function, suspect that the battery charge is low. Try hand starting, if available. If the engine will not turn, there may be water in the cylinders. Corroded battery connections or insecure connections to the starter motor may be the trouble.

If the battery is in good condition, the starter or switch may be faulty. If the starter motor whines, but will not engage, free the sliding pinion.

The above faults may be present to a lesser extent if the engine only turns slowly. A fully charged battery is the most important consideration.

If the engine turns, but does not fire, the fault is in the ignition or the fuel system. Check ignition by removing a lead and hold it by its insulation near the plug and look for a spark. If there is no spark, check security of cable joints in the starting circuit. Look for dampness, particularly at the distributor.

If there is a spark at a plug, check that petrol is being fed to the carburettor. Check that the choke is working. If there is no fuel at the carburettor, check that there is fuel in the tank. If there is a pump, check that it is working. If electric, check its electrical connections. A sharp tap may free a sticking pump.

If there is an excess of fuel shown at the carburettor and the engine has been turning for some time without firing, it will be necessary to clean and dry the plugs. The carburettor should be checked for the cause of flooding.

Running problems
If the engine starts, but stalls when idling before it has warmed up, the choke may not be operating correctly and may need adjustment. If the engine will not idle when it has warmed, the fuel mixture may be wrong, an idling jet in the carburettor may be blocked, the choke may still be closed or the engine

idling speed may be adjusted too low.

If the engine stalls when accelerated the supply of fuel to the engine is probably inadequate due to a fault in the carburettor. Blocked filters may be holding up supply. Poor acceleration is due to the same causes, or the valves may need adjusting or grinding.

Lack of power may be due to insufficient fuel, too weak a mixture, incorrect ignition timing, worn or badly adjusted valves, or the wrong grade of fuel.

If the engine misses, look for loose electrical connections, worn distributor points, dirt in the carburettor or low fuel in the carburettor.

If the reason for a fault is not immediately obvious and the engine is known to have run before, test possible causes one at a time and return the particular thing to the state it was before moving to another test. Work from the simplest things first. The cause of a fault is more likely to be something capable of a simple remedy than one requiring a major adjustment. At least, start with that assumption and eliminate all the possible simple causes before tackling any work involving dismantling or the use of special tools. If there is a spark and fuel, the engine should run, even if not satisfactorily, but having made it run the cause of irregularities may be sought and eliminated.

If there has been too enthusiastic use of the starter motor, so the cylinders and plugs are flooded, besides drying plugs it may be advisable to wait a while before attempting another start.

see also BATTERY; ENGINE ELECTRICAL SYSTEM; FUEL SYSTEM; IGNITION SYSTEM; INBOARD ENGINES, PETROL; OUTBOARD MOTORS.

Inflatable boats (Fig. 30)

Only the simpler inflatable playboats are made of natural rubber. Yachts' dinghies are made of synthetic rubber (neoprene). This is less affected by oil and other things on or in the water, but it is still advisable to clean an inflatable boat frequently. A freshwater hose may be all that is needed. Sand and grit may be sucked out of folds and angles of a dry boat by a vacuum cleaner. It is unwise to use a vacuum cleaner to deflate the boat as there may be moisture as well as air, which could damage the cleaner or be dangerous if in contact with its electrical parts. Oil on the boat skin may be cleaned off with white spirit.

If the boat is to be stored briefly, it is probably better kept inflated. If it is to be packed and stored for a longer time, make sure the skin is both clean and dry. Check that any rope is also dry and that there is no sand trapped where it is attached. Wooden parts should be stored separately. Make sure wood has its edges rounded and that there are no broken or splintered fibres that could damage the skin. Keep the wood varnished or painted to prevent water absorption. The stored boat may have to be kept in its valise or container for convenience, but if it can be left more loosely packed for a long storage it is less likely to develop tight folds and creases, which are where leaks tend to develop in an older boat.

If damage is in the form of a definite

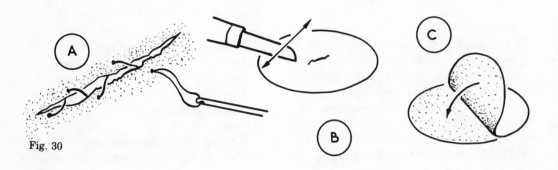

Fig. 30

hole, it is more easily located and dealt with than when the leak is general or minor. If an inflated compartment can be pushed under water, air leaking can be seen as bubbles and the spot marked. If this cannot be done, soapy water may be spread with a broad brush and bubbles looked for. If there are leaks in the flexible floor, have the inside absolutely dry, then float the boat and press the bottom down so water is forced through any hole, which can be marked for repair after drying.

Most makers provide a repair kit and this should be used if possible. Otherwise, make sure the repair material is neoprene and the adhesive is one intended for that material. Ordinary rubber solution is unsuitable. There are plugs for temporary repairs, but for a more permanent repair a patch should be stuck on and this should be given a good overlap of the damage. A patch with rounded corners is likely to stay put better than one with sharp corners, which may tend to curl away. Having the whole patch with curved edges is probably better than straight sides with rounded corners, but not necessarily a true circle or ellipse.

If the damage is large or ragged, pull the edges together with a few large stitches (A) to take any expanding strain from the patch. Mark the outline of the patch with chalk or a chinagraph pencil so adhesive is not spread unnecessarily and messily. Make sure the patch and the area it is to cover are clean. Using coarse abrasive paper or scraping with a knife blade will expose a new surface (B). Spread adhesive thinly on the skin and the patch. Read the directions. It will probably have to be left at least one-quarter hour to become almost dry. Bring the patch into position and press it down – get it right the first time, and lower on from one side so no air is trapped (C). Rub down with something hard, working from the middle of the patch outwards. For anything but an emergency repair, leave the repair to cure for a day before inflating and using the boat.

If there is no obvious leak in the skin, suspect the valves before testing for other leaks. Immerse the valve or test it with soapy water introduced with a small brush and worked around as far as can be reached.

If testing shows a general porosity, the skin material is deteriorating. If it is localized, a large patch may provide a cure, but when the boat is reaching this state, it may be better to return it to the makers for advice and servicing. Over-inflation may cause a breakdown of proofing leading to porosity. A compartment should not be inflated more than is obviously necessary to hold its shape. Powered inflation should be used with caution.

Some paints will either not adhere or may attack an inflatable boat skin. If a name or other marking is to be put on an inflatable boat, only use a paint intended for the material.

Inhibiting

If machinery, metal accessories and similar things are to be left for some time unused, it is advisable to protect them, in most cases by coating with an oil sold as a spray or brush-on machinery preservative. Lubricating oil will not do. Preservative oil should only be used on a surface and kept out of such things as mast grooves, insides of blocks and other recesses.

If an engine can be turned over or run briefly every six weeks or so, special internal treatment may be unnecessary. The pistons and cylinders particularly need protection. Remove spark plugs or injectors. Squirt in a little light oil and turn the engine over a few times. Squirt in a little more, then seal with corks or old spark plugs. Sump oil ought to be changed before lay-up. Carburettors are better taken home if the boat is to remain elsewhere.

An outboard motor needs a generally similar treatment. If it has been used in salt water, run it in fresh water to flush it. Keep the motor the right way up. Turn it over by hand to remove water. See that any water in the gearbox is forced out by filling completely with oil or grease.

If external moving parts, particularly screws, are to be protected and prevented from seizing during a long storage, use stern gland or water pump grease, instead of ordinary lubricants.

Insulators

Many non-conducting materials are used for electrical insulation, but most are now plastic, although rubber, glazed earthenware and other materials are used. Dry wood has reasonable insulating qualities. Water is a good conductor, so wood that has absorbed moisture loses its insulating qualities.

Any good insulating material is liable to lose some of its qualities in a salty atmosphere. Salt deposited on the surface attracts moisture, so the thin film of dampness allows electricity to leak. Cracks harbour moisture and cause electrical leaks. Insulators for radio and other purposes used externally should be cleaned frequently. If the backstay is used as an aerial the lower insulator is particularly liable to become salty. Wiping with a dry cloth should be enough, although in a bad case it can be moistened with a cleaning fluid. Spraying with a drying and insulating fluid may delay further trouble, but salt will settle on this and attract moisture to cause a further electrical leak.

Insulating panels used for electrical work anywhere in a boat should be wiped occasionally between metal contacts mounted on them, in case salt has settled. Even away from a salty atmosphere, dust containing metal particles may cause trouble.

Kapok

At one time kapok was used as a buoyancy material. It is a vegetable fibre that has plenty of buoyancy when dry, but it absorbs water and then loses its buoyancy. Some later buoyancy garments had kapok sealed in plastic sheaths to prevent water absorption, but kapok has now been replaced by closed-cell plastic foam, which has none of kapok's drawbacks. Any safety equipment containing kapok should be discarded and replaced with modern equipment to conform to the latest knowledge and recommendations.

Keels

The main concern with a keel is its security, whether it is a deep central fin keel or bilge keel. A wooden keel may be built into the wooden hull by building up laminations with comparatively little load on fastenings, but if there is a ballast keel, the loads on bolts and other fastenings can be considerable.

The direct weight of a ballast keel is usually taken by long bolts. These may corrode and their effective thickness be reduced. Without equipment that is not readily available, the only way to check the condition of a bolt is to withdraw it. If a deep keel boat has been in use for some years it is advisable to withdraw a sample bolt and inspect it. If this has corroded, others should be tested. Failure of the bolts at sea could mean the loss of the ballast keel and possibly loss of the ship.

Besides the direct weight due to gravity, fastenings have to take large wracking loads when a keel is doing its job of preventing leeway when sailing with a beam wind. Fastenings through keels or the flanges of bilge keels should show no sign of movement inside the hull. If they do, loads are better spread with steel plates than with washers. Most large strains are crosswise, so the plates may extend over packings arranged each side of the line of fastenings.

Because keels have to provide support for the boat when hauled out they only get indifferent attention. If the boat can be raised enough for the keel to clear the ground or a pit dug below the keel, its bottom may be examined for plugs over bolt ends, fairing off can be done if it is damaged, and anti-fouling can be applied to its bottom as well as the sides.

As a keel is drawn through deeper and more 'solid' water, smoothness and streamlining are more important than with higher hull parts. When repainting, get the surface as smooth as possible. If a rudder and/or propeller follow the keel, see that they blend into the keel and the edge of the keel is faired to give a free flow of water past the propeller.

A dinghy gets its sailing keel surface from a centreboard, but there is a smaller central projection forming a keel for most of the length of the hull, which acts as a keel when the boat is ashore and may serve to maintain direction when the boat is rowed or under power. If the keel is of unprotected wood, any wear should be cleaned smooth and new paint or varnish applied.

In many cases there is a half-round metal moulding that may continue around the stem. Fastenings through this tend to get pulled when the boat is dragged. Check their security. If the strip is worn, countersink the screw heads more. Holes may have to be plugged or longer screws used.

In some sailing dinghies the metal strip divides around the centreboard slot and holds a rubber flap over the slot. If this has to be replaced, put it on in one piece. Punch screw holes, if possible, otherwise the action of driving screws buckles the rubber. After the rubber has been fixed all round, cut the slot with a knife.

see also ANTI-FOULING; CENTRE AND DAGGER BOARDS.

Kicking strap

Where tackle is used to pull the boom down, the load when the boat is sailed hard is heavy on both the tackle and its fastenings. The pull should come from as low as possible on the mast and the angle of the kicking strap is usually slightly more upright than 45 degrees, so as not to interfere with the crew or other equipment, but the further the pull comes from the mast, within reason, the better will the sail set.

If the lower part is riveted to the foot of a metal mast it is unlikely that fastenings will have moved, but if there are wood screws, check their security, and either use larger screws or plug the holes if there is any loosening. Check the fastenings of the keyhole plate or other attachment on the boom. Examine splices or other attachments of the tackle. There may be wear or bending of pins. Shackles or thimbles may have distorted under load. If part of the tackle is stainless steel wire rope, this is unlikely to have deteriorated, but the fibre rope part of the tackle may have the tension maintained by a jamb cleat. Examine the rope for wear or damage at the point where it is usually gripped. Move the rope, alter its length or turn it end for end so wear comes at a different place, if the line has not yet reached the stage where it would be better replaced.

see also RIGGING, RUNNING.

Knees (Fig. 31)

Traditional wooden boats have many wooden brackets, with several names according to position, but collectively known as knees. They have uses in plywood and other constructions, particularly quarter knees between transom and gunwales and a breasthook between the gunwales at the stem. A traditional knee was 'grown oak', meaning it was cut where grain followed its shape, for greatest strength (A). Such a piece of wood is unlikely to be available for a replacement, and the alternative, which is stronger, is a laminated knee (B).

One way of making laminated knees is to pull many thin strips of wood around a can or other round object, with glue between and cramp until set (C). This is backed up by a small solid block of wood and the whole thing cut to shape (D). Extra strength can be built in if the prepared knee is given a curve to blend into the surfaces it meets, then after

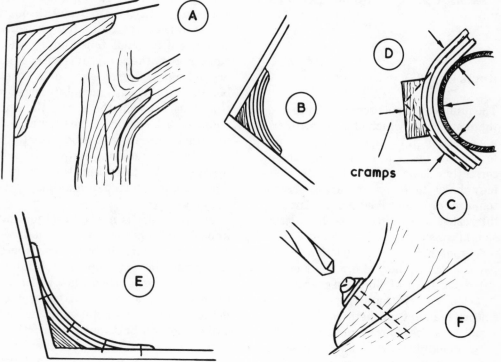

cramps

Fig. 31

fixing, another lamination is added, with a few nails or other fastenings to pull it in while the glue sets, and ends which extend (E).

Traditional knees were only held by copper nails and roves. If a broken knee is to be removed, centre-punch the riveted end of nail and drill through the rove (F). The remains of the nail can then be driven out. A modern knee is better held with glue and sufficient screws to pull the parts together while the glue sets.

see also CLINKER PLANKING; LAMINAT-ING.

Knots (Fig. 32)

The number of knots seems infinite and there are books which offer a bewildering selection. It is important in boating to know a few knots and apply them correctly. Some essential knots that may have to be used during maintenance are described here. Anyone interested in knotting as a subject should consult a specialist book.

A knot holds by the friction of its parts on each other. Many knots originated for natural fibre rope are also suitable for synthetic rope, but for smooth filament synthetic rope there is sometimes a need for extra turns to produce enough friction. A knot is a weak point in a rope. A test to destruction would result in a break at a knot. The best knots are those that produce the minimum weakening. If knots can be avoided, they should, if the rope is under considerable strain. A well-made splice should be stronger than any knot.

The simplest knot is the overhand or thumb (A). If something bigger is needed to prevent the rope pulling through the hand or a hole, take the end around the other side before passing through to make the figure-eight knot (B).

The basic joining knot is the sheet bend (common bend). Turn one part back and work the other end through and around this bight (C). It is probably stronger if the ends finish on opposite sides. For synthetic rope it is wiser to go around again to make a double sheet bend (D). If there is much difference in thickness between the parts, the one doubled back should be the thicker and the other end can go around more than twice before tucking. With this and many other knots, making the last tuck with a bight of the rope allows easy casting off (E).

The reef knot is not the best joining knot for all occasions as is sometimes thought. It is not suitable for use where the loaded knot is unsupported, but it is suitable if the finished knot will bear against something, as in tying reef points (from which it takes its name). Twist the two parts over each other, then make the second twist the other way so each end will lie alongside its

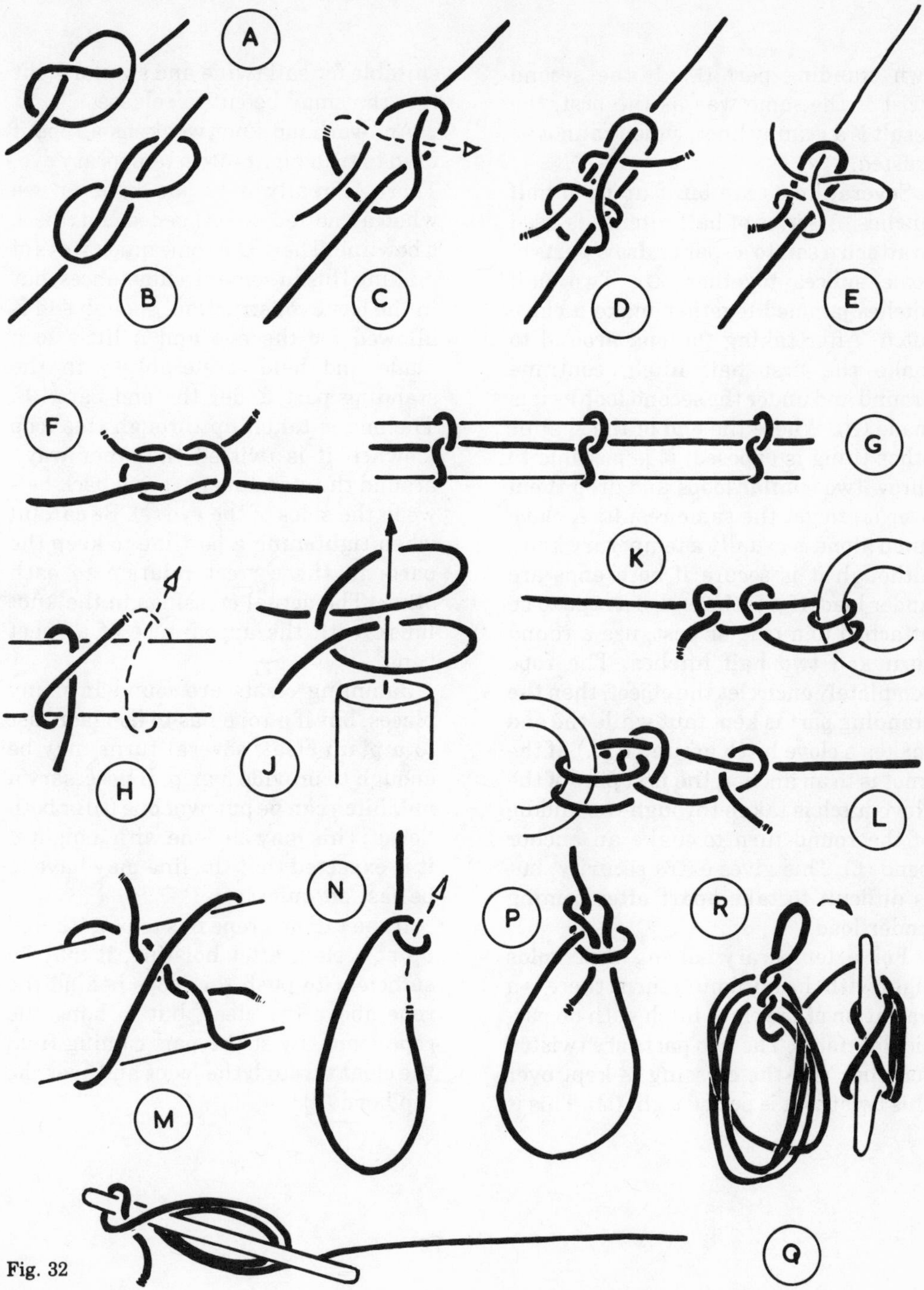

Fig. 32

own standing part (F). If the second twist is the same way as the first, the result is a granny knot, which cannot be trusted.

Several knots are built up from half hitches. A series of half hitches is used to attach a sail to a spar or draw parts of some splices together (G). Two half hitches jammed together make a clove hitch. After taking the end around to make the first half hitch, continue around and under the second loop as it is made (H). Where the end of the spar or other thing is exposed, it is possible to throw two similar loops and drop them over (J) to get the same result. A clove hitch alone is usually a temporary knot, although it is secure if both ends are under load. If it is the end of a rope to be attached to a ring or post, use a round turn and two half hitches. The rope completely encircles the object, then the standing part is kept taut while the end makes a clove hitch around it (K). If the knot is to an anchor, the first part of the clove hitch is taken through the middle of the round turn to make an anchor bend (L). This gives extra security, but is difficult to take apart after coming under load.

For a temporary seizing that holds tight with the minimum turns there is a variation of the clove hitch with no particular name. The two parts are twisted together and the crossing is kept over this twist as it is pulled tight (M). This is suitable for sail twine and similar light line that may be cut to release.

An overhand knot weakens a rope if used to tie a bight into a temporary eye. There is really only one knot to use when a knotted eye is needed and this is a bowline. There are some quick ways of making this in some circumstances, but in the basic construction, enough end is allowed for the eye and a little loop made and held, preferably with the standing part under the end part (N). The end is taken up through this loop (down if it is twisted the other way), around the standing part and back between the sides of the eye (P). Be careful when tightening a bowline to keep the parts in the correct relation to each other. The actual crossings in the knot finish with the appearance of a sheet bend.

Jamming cleats are found in many places, but if a rope has to be made fast to a plain cleat, several turns may be enough to provide a grip. If necessary a half hitch can be put over one (Q) or both horns. This may be done with a bight if it is expected that the line may have to be cast off quickly.

If the tail of a rope has to be gathered up at a cleat after hoisting, it may be sufficient to push the loops behind the rope above the cleat, but to hang the rope loops, twist the part coming from the cleat through the loops and over the top horn (R).

Lacing (Fig. 33)

Old natural fibre lacing line may be replaced with braided synthetic line. Sealing the ends with heat may be sufficient to prevent fraying, but it will make threading easier if the free end is also tightly whipped. As this braided line cannot be spliced, a loop in the other end may be seized. Synthetic line is much more slippery than natural line. In places where a simple over-and-over threading has been used, a better grip and tension will be obtained by half-hitching. This is particularly so when attaching a sail to a spar or drawing the edges of a cover together.

Laminating (Fig. 34)

One advantage of the availability of waterproof synthetic resin wood glues of ample strength is that it is possible to build up parts instead of cut them from solid wood. Besides being less wasteful of materials, the result is usually a stronger article, as lines of grain follow the shape, instead of some being severed when a curved part is cut from solid wood. Some information on laminating particular parts is given elsewhere, but the general method is described here.

It is sometimes possible to laminate in position, but it is more usual to make a laminated part independently. The wood may be in any thickness from veneer upwards. Thick pieces cannot be sprung to tight curves. Some woods bend more easily than others. If a laminated article has to hold much curve, there should be at least three laminations, whatever the total thickness. It is usual for all laminations to be the same thickness. This is convenient, but not

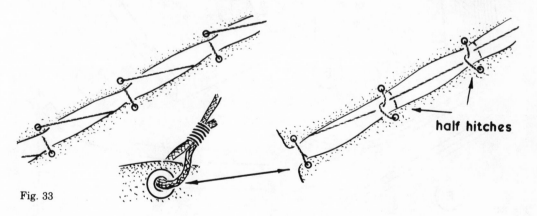

half hitches

Fig. 33

essential to success. Using different coloured woods provides decoration, and this is often done in dinghy tillers.

The wood used in laminating should have planed surfaces. If already machine-planed it is advisable to follow by hand planing to remove any case-hardening of the surface by blunt machine blades, which would not absorb glue. Coarse sanding would have a similar cleaning effect, but be careful of rounding edges. It may also help to pull a fine saw blade sideways over the surface to make a pattern of fine scratches to help glue penetration.

The glue used may be any of the wood glues used elsewhere in boat building, with epoxy producing the strongest results. There are no flexible wood glues of sufficient strength, so the effect of gluing laminations is to produce an article that will be stiffer than if made from solid wood. If there are any open or failed joints, these tend to be at ends.

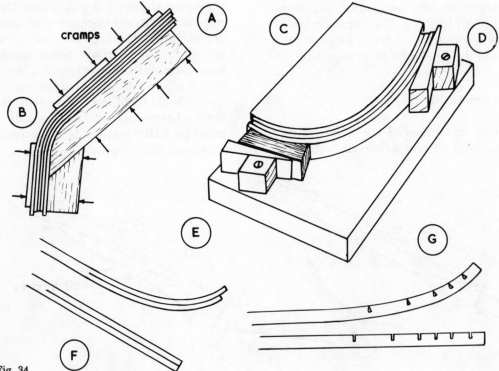

cramps

Fig. 34

100

Because of this it is usual to make any laminated construction longer than finally needed so the waste ends can be cut off.

A former of sufficient rigidity is needed to hold parts to the intended shape. For a simple shape, like a stem, it can be built up from stout scrap wood (A). Its face width should be more than the width of the lamination. Its thickness must be enough for stiffness, but not so much that cramps cannot be used. Cramps should have thin scrap wood to spread the pressure and reduce marking of the wood (B). They will have to be closer where the curve is greatest. Excess length does not matter and for many things the edges need not be an exact match if there is enough allowed for planing after the glue has set. Avoid excessive pressure on the cramps. They must pull the parts to shape and bring the glued surfaces into close contact, but squeezing after that stage may force out glue, so not enough is left to make a good joint.

For lighter work and more complex shapes, the shaped part of the former may be on a baseboard (C) and pressure, in some parts at least, applied by wedges (D). This suits a lamination made up from a large number of thin pieces of wood. The wedge may press directly on the wood or shaped blocks may be used (E) to get a better spread of pressure on a curve.

It is difficult to avoid surplus glue getting on to the former or other places where it is not wanted. Paper on the former prevents sticking and can be scraped off the laminated part later. Greasing the former will also prevent sticking, but this leaves the laminated part greasy as well.

Laminated parts may be used with solid parts. There is no need to build up a thick section with many laminations at a point where a solid block would be just as effective. This may happen in a knee, where the final point is a solid piece glued to the curved laminations. The end of a tiller may have to be thickened to fit into the rudder head, and this can be built up with solid pieces. A thickening at the other end of the tiller, to prevent the hand slipping off, may be built up with solid blocks, then worked to shape. Shaped parts through several thicknesses will give an attractive appearance of grain pattern, even if different coloured woods are not used.

Not strictly laminating, but a way to get a bend into a solid part that resists curving without treatment, is to make one or two lengthwise cuts with a circular saw, using a fine blade. The saw kerfs are sprung open to allow glue to be spread, then the wood pulled to shape and held until the glue has set (F). The other way to persuade wood to take a tight curve is to make a series of saw cuts across it (G), but as this severs grain fibres it weakens the wood.

see also ADHESIVES; FRAMES AND TIMBERS; KNEES; RUDDER.

Launching trolley

The trolley used for handling a dinghy in and out of the water is usually simple and cheap with plain bearings. Dismantle each wheel bearing occasionally and fill with water pump or stern shaft grease. Wash salt off as often as possible. If the steel frame rusts, treat it with rust-inhibiting fluid and repaint it before the rust has made much progress.

Check the supports for the dinghy. They should match the dinghy, otherwise it may be marked or damaged when wheeled over a rough surface. Broad bearing surfaces are advisable. If possible, the supports should fit around chines or other parts to prevent movement. Padding should be adequate as most trolleys are unsprung. Marking with the name of the boat or fixing a name and address label may be worthwhile.

Legs

If a fin-keel boat carries legs to help it sit upright when it takes the bottom, it is important that they should be strong and secure. Check the bottoms of old legs for signs of rot. If the bottoms are worn, reinforcing pieces may be scarfed or bolted on. At the top there may be a bolt through the gunwale, but the load should be taken by parts that bear against each other. Check these for security and wear. Build up where necessary. Oak or similar water-resistant strong hardwood should be used. If there are guys fore and aft from the legs, see that the rope used is sound, splices or other attachments are holding and the anchorages to both leg and gunwale are secure. There can be considerable strain in many directions during the period when a boat with legs takes the bottom or lifts off with a rising tide. Check that the attachment points are able to take racking strains in several directions. Increasing the area that bears against the hull may be advisable.

Lifebuoys (lifebelts, life rings)

The word 'lifebelt' is now assumed to be something to throw to a person in the water, not something which is worn – that is, a 'lifejacket' or 'buoyancy aid', collectively known as personal buoyancy. Older lifebelts or lifebuoys were made of cork. More recent ones are of plastic. The traditional type favoured on British craft is a full circle, but U-shaped ones are found in some countries.

A lifebelt may have lines attached to it by canvas bands. Check that the whole lifebelt is sound. If it is canvas-covered, the interior can be felt. Attempt to flex the material. This will show any cracks inside. Slight occasional cracks may not matter, but if the material seems to be disintegrating to loose particles, it will no longer function properly and may soon lose its shape. Check the state of the lines and the canvas bands retaining them. Older lifebelts may have natural fibre lines which have rotted and should be replaced with synthetic rope. Avoid the stiffer synthetics. A flexible rope is easier for a person in the water to handle.

If there is a flare or light attached to the lifebuoy, check that the lanyard is secure at both ends and has not deteriorated or been chafed. It may be possible to check a lamp without destroying it, depending on its type, but the only way to check a flare is to use it. An old flare, which is near or past the date specified by the makers, should certainly be replaced. If it is then fired, do it somewhere that cannot be interpreted by anyone as a disaster at sea!

A lifebuoy is often painted with the name of its ship and its home port. This is a good idea, but the painted ring is often used more as a decorative feature on small craft than as a safety device. Its mounting on board should have accessibility for use in emergency as a first consideration. In a small forward-cabin cruiser, having the lifebuoy resting on brackets on the top of the cabin is a good idea. Anyone looking from above can read the name and the ring is easily reached if it has to be thrown.

Any stowage should allow the ring to be lifted without the need to unfasten catches, release tied lines or do anything except reach for the lifebuoy. If not flat, there may be shaped hooks or a framework into which the lifebuoy drops. If the present stowage is otherwise or non-existent, it should be modified. It is important that a lifebuoy has a known place, where it can be found without searching.

To be used for a person in the water to get his head and shoulders through, a lifebuoy has to be larger than can be stowed conveniently in small craft. A smaller version may have uses, but reducing the size reduces the buoyancy and some of the smallest lifebuoys are not really practicable, although they may make good decorations. An alternative for the smallest craft is a buoyant cushion. If the helmsman always sits on it, he has it readily to hand to throw if anyone goes overboard.

see also PERSONAL BUOYANCY.

Limber holes

Water in the bottom of any boat should be able to run to the lowest point where it can be bailed or pumped out. Any parts of the framing or structure close to the skin should have holes at their lowest point so water can run through. These limber holes should be checked to ensure that they remain clear. Any solid debris that has got into the bilges should be cleared from the holes, otherwise trapped water may become stagnant giving unpleasant smells and encouraging rot. Washing through with clean water and detergent will show if the holes are strategically placed, or whether new holes will have to be made.

see also BILGE PUMPS.

Lubricants

Where one thing moves on another, lubrication reduces friction and therefore makes for efficiency. Where a mechanical system or an arrangement of blocks and rope to form tackle are used, the losses due to friction are considerably less with good lubrication than with dry bearings. Unfortunately, the use of lubricants in some circumstances may damage or deface nearby materials, but the correct choice of lubricant reduces this problem.

Some bearings are impregnated with lubricant and do not need attention. These may be metal or plastic. Some plastic sheaves and other wheels operate successfully without lubrication. There are water-lubricated bearings for underwater situations, such as the propeller shaft.

Motor lubrication should follow makers' recommendations. These oils are sometimes the same as those intended for car engines, but for some motors the oil must be a single-grade type and the multi-grade types used in many cars are unsuitable. Follow the maker's advice for the underwater gearbox of an outboard motor. The risk of water entering makes it important that a suitable oil or grease is used. When topping up during maintenance do not mix lubricants. The amount involved is small and it may be wiser to drain and refill with new lubricant.

For general lubrication of things about the boat that are not equipped with nipples or the means of force-feeding lubricant, a pump-action oilcan with cycle oil or car oil of about 20-grade should do. A thin oil will penetrate, but it may soon be worked out of the bearing. If a thicker oil can be forced in, it should remain effective longer. For lubrication points with nipples for a grease gun, a thick oil should be used for a bearing of modest size, but if it is more extensive, like a cable in a casing, a thinner oil will spread better. For screw-down greasers, quite thick grease can be used, filled to the top and screwed down at regular intervals. How much to screw down and how often will be found by experience. Excessive screwing down will force grease out of the bearing and a rotating shaft may throw it around.

Where less messy lubricants are needed, there are other things. Graphite will lubricate. This may be in an oil or grease, then the graphite is left after oil has dispersed. Pencils are graphite. Rubbering a sticking zip fastener with a pencil may be all that is needed to lubricate the parts without soiling adjoining parts. Candle wax will also act as a lubricant for similar things. Beeswax or a wax polish can be used on sliding surfaces. Do not use varnish. Soap also is a useful lubricant for rubber; either rubber to rubber or to another material. Rubber moulding for windows or similar may be lubricated with soapy water to ease assembly.

Masking tape

This is a useful material to use when painting. It is paper self-adhesive tape which does not leave a sticky surface when peeled off. If a sharp line is needed between two colours, paint one and allow it to dry. It may taper over the intended final meeting line. Lay a line of masking tape with its edge on the intended line and paint the other colour. With some paints, the tape can be left until they are dry, then the tape peeled off. With those that set very hard, particularly some two-pot types, the tape should be peeled before the paint has fully hardened, otherwise any that has run over the tape may crack instead of leaving a clean line.

If paint is to be sprayed, use masking tape to hold paper over any parts that have to be protected from the spray, but let the tape outline the sprayed area to give a clean border.

Masking tape has other uses. It can be stretched around parts that have to be held together while glue or other adhesive sets. It can be used to temporarily bundle things together. It will make temporary labels. However, it should be kept away from water. For damp situations use self-adhesive waterproof plastic strip.

see also ADHESIVE TAPE.

Masts (Fig. 35)

Wooden masts are mostly made of softwoods, for lightness, and these are not very durable. Check the foot of a mast if stepped on the hog, for rot and wear. It may be possible to cut off the end and scarf on a new piece. The foot of such a mast can be treated with two-part varnish, a mastic preparation or other fully waterproof treatment to prevent the entry of water. Elsewhere, keep the mast varnished.

If a wooden mast is stored horizontally when the boat is out of commission support it evenly at fairly close intervals and turn it occasionally during storage. It is best under cover so it is protected from rain, but avoid close wrapping. There should be a good flow of air around it.

Even a dinghy mast is top-heavy if attempts are made to lift it out by hand. If a small boat can be turned on its side, the mast may be more safely removed or replaced near a horizontal position. If it has to be lifted vertically, arrange the lift to come from above its centre of gravity, by a crane, sheer legs or a high dockside. If a mast falls, the damage done to it is liable to be serious.

Softwood does not provide a good grip for screws. Check all fastenings. If thicker screws cannot be used, plug worn holes and re-enter the screws. Longer screws are not usually advisable, particularly if the mast is hollow and the points may go through.

It is possible to scarf-in reinforcing pieces at points of chafe or wear. They can be harder wood. Let the ends of any pieces finish in a long bevel to give a good grip for glue. Make a piece oversize and shape it afterwards (A).

If the head of a wood mast is without a truck or cap, see that the end grain is thoroughly impregnated with waterproof varnish or synthetic resin glue.

A metal mast may need little treatment, but check the security of all fastenings and wash off salt, then store it in the same way as recommended for a wooden mast. If an aluminium mast has been anodized it should be satisfactory without treatment. Corrosion of a plain aluminium mast can be prevented by treating with car wax polish. If there is the rough surface and white dust of corrosion, use fine abrasive before waxing.

With a larger and older yacht the mast passing through the deck may be wedged there. Although support from the wedges is an essential part of the design, get the mast rake correctly adjusted with its stays, then drive wedges opposite each other so as to grip the mast without forcing it out of shape.

The opening in the deck may be protected by a mast coat, which is more easy to renew after the mast has been taken out. If the old one cannot be used as a pattern, draw the intended side

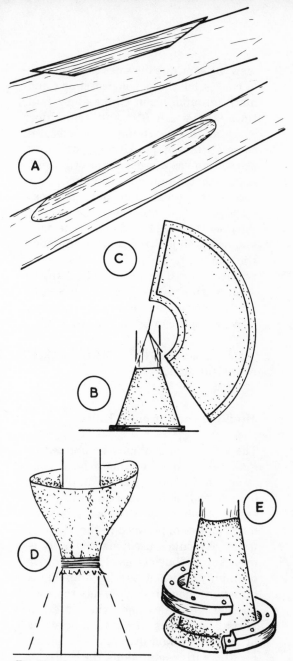

Fig. 35

view (B), continue the sides to the centre of curves for the developed shape and mark around about three-and-a-half times the width (C). Add something spare at the edges and cut a piece of canvas to this shape. Although ordinary proofed canvas was usual and still used, plastic-coated fabric is suitable.

Sew the seam and put the coat upside-down on the mast and seize it securely (D). Pull this down to the deck and bed it on jointing compound under the old ring. If the ring has to be replaced, it can be a continuous ring of stout marine plywood, if it can be put in place before the mast is stepped. Otherwise, it can be in two parts (E).

see also FASTENINGS; HALYARDS; SCARFING; SPARS.

Moulded (hot or cold) hulls

The word 'moulded' may be applied to glassfibre and other methods of construction. In boats it is normally used for a method of building up a hull with strips of veneer so the result is very much a piece of plywood in the shape of a boat. A mould is used, made of battens over frames, but not as close-fitting or as highly finished as the plug for a glassfibre moulding. This has recesses for hog, gunwales and other internal parts. These parts are put in, then strips of veneer are laid diagonally in place, usually with a joint along the centre of

the hog. Staples are used to hold the strips in place. They are glued to any structural members. Polythene sheeting prevents adhesion to the mould. Another layer of veneers is put on, sloping the opposite way to the first with glue between the layers and earlier staples withdrawn as new ones are driven. When the glue of this layer has set, its staples are withdrawn and a third layer fitted. For a canoe the veneers may be only 1 mm thick. For a dinghy they would be about 3 mm and for a larger craft they might be thicker or consist of more layers.

There is considerable strength in the skin of such a hull and little or no internal framework is needed. 'Hot' or 'cold' only indicate the method of setting the glue. Heat and pressure may be used in production work, but in cold moulding the glue sets at normal temperatures.

Damage to a moulded hull is localized as the crossing veneers limit splitting or spreading. It is possible to let in wood, as described for plywood repairs. Veneer layers may be cut away in differing amounts and new veneers glued in. Simplest and quite satisfactory for a small hole is glassfibre and resin, as described for glassfibre repairs.

This method can be used for other things besides hulls. A curved cabin edge can be made over a simple mould. There are dinghies with plywood panels for bottoms and sides, but with moulded sections for bilges, instead of the usual hard chines.

Navigation lights (Fig. 36)

Port and starboard lights are often mounted incorrectly. Whatever their type they should be parallel with the waterline, their inner surface upright and the beam controlled so it shows from directly ahead to 'two points abaft the beam'. Small navigation lights on a cabin side are often toed-in and not level. It is better to give them light boards, which can be painted appropriately and blocks of wood included that restrict the beam to the correct angles.

Nets (Fig. 37)

Nearly all nets, whether hand or machine made, have the meshes formed with sheet bends (A). With synthetic line, which is more slippery than natural fibre line, a knot may become upset (B). This allows the knot to slip and the meshes to distort. A knot can be coaxed back into position and reshaped with the aid of a spike.

If the net has been broken, it will almost certainly be necessary to cut away the damage so new line can be worked in a continuous piece. Examine a knot and turn the net so the knots are the right way up (A). Cut away the damaged parts so you have a 'three-legged mesh' to start at (C) and can follow rows across, going backwards and forwards enough to take care of the damage. This means cutting so there are meshes to join at the ends of rows and another three-legged mesh to finish on. If it is a single row, the repair pattern is a simple zigzag, but for more extensive damage it is helpful to put a rod through sound meshes above the damage and map out how the repair will go (D). If the meshes are arranged as a diamond pattern, the rod will be parallel to a side of the net, but if it is a square pattern the rod is parallel to the diamond form in which the meshes were made, so is diagonal to the edge (E).

Along upper meshes, broken pieces can be pulled out to leave the plain loop of the remaining mesh, but elsewhere short ends should be left (F). Make sure all knotted short ends are tight.

A few meshes can be made without tools, but if many are to be made it is a help to have a gauge, which is merely a

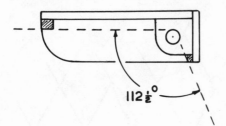

$112\frac{1}{2}°$

Fig. 36

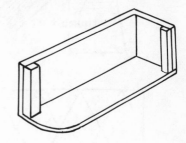

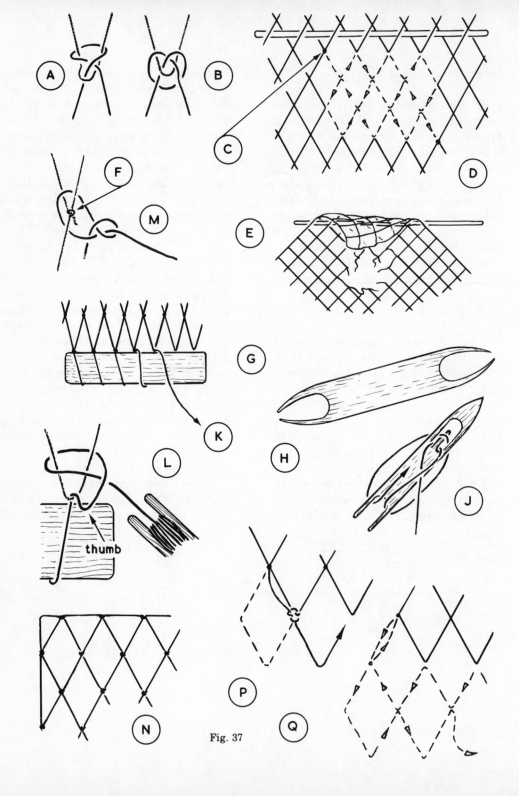

Fig. 37

thin piece of wood with rounded corners and a width equal to half the depth of a mesh (G). To gather up the line being used a netmaker uses a needle, which can be made of wood for larger meshes, but there are metal and plastic ones for fine work. One version has open ends and the line merely wraps around (H). Another has a point and the line goes around a peg from alternate sides (J).

To make a mesh, the gauge is held against the bottom of the one above, the line brought down the front and up the back to come forward through the mesh (K). It is held by the thumb on the gauge and the needle taken around the back, across the front and under its own loop (L). Let the part go from under the thumb and pull the knot tight (A). Watch that it does not become upset (B) in tightening. In a row of meshes, the one just formed is allowed to slide along the gauge and the next one is made in the same way.

For a repair, tie the end to the three-legged mesh. This can be a sheet bend, but it is simpler to use a figure-eight knot (M). Follow across, making a row of meshes. If it is only a single row, similar knots will have to be made alternately to the sound meshes below. If there is more than one new row needed, go down at the end of the first row to join into the side of a sound mesh, ready to start back on the next row. This can be a sheet bend worked to the side. Although it is possible to reverse all the actions and go back from right to left, most workers prefer to turn the net over, so the next row is done left to right again. After sufficient rows, finish with a figure-eight knot at the last three-legged mesh.

Edges of nets are finished in several ways. If damage reaches an edge an examination of the existing edge will show the treatment and diamond-mesh nets may be worked straight across to make an edge (N) or the meshes may be seized or knotted to a bolt rope. With square mesh it is necessary to add a mesh at one end of a row and remove one at the other end as the meshes are worked diagonally.

At the end where a mesh has to be lost, take the line down to the bottom of the mesh just formed and knot it there (P), then continue the shortened row below. If a mesh has to be added to a row, go up to the side of the last old mesh and knot there, then come down to knot into the side of the mesh just made (Q), ready to start back on a new lengthened row.

An expert netmaker works with the net gathered up and the meshes hanging almost straight down. This may be done after some experience has been gained, but it is easier to get a repair exact to size if the work is opened out to approximately the shape the meshes take in use. The techniques described are satisfactory for most nets, but if the synthetic line is very slippery, go twice around at the starting and finishing knots.

Oars (Fig. 38)

Although other materials are sometimes used, the majority of oars are made of wood. Oars for use on the sea were traditionally made of ash, which is springy and able to stand up to the stresses of rowing strongly in broken water, but oars for use on inland waters have usually been made of spruce or other softwood and these are commonly used on the sea as well today.

Ash does not absorb water as readily as a softwood and its blade is less likely to split. Because of this, traditional ash oars were not usually varnished and there was no protection at the tip. If ash oars have to be serviced, it may only be necessary to clean off raggedness at the ends and sand rough surfaces, although a much-worn oar may get some or all of the treatment described for softwood oars. Ash oars are extremely heavy compared with softwood oars. If they are to be replaced, softwood oars are advised and any odd ash oar can be kept for sculling over the stern – an activity which tends to wear any oar, but for which the springiness of ash is an advantage.

Unprotected softwood tends to absorb water very readily. If an otherwise satisfactory oar needs revarnishing and has bare patches of wood showing, allow it some time to dry out, particularly at any exposed end grain. The tip of the blade will probably be last to dry out. It is usual to leave the grip (A) unvarnished, so the hand does not slip, but this ought to be sanded smooth at the same time as there is any rubbing down of old varnish. Softwood tends to become ragged and splintery. If there is roughness where the oar has taken knocks, use a scraper in both directions before sanding. Fibres tend to turn over and stand up again later, if sanding only is used. The scraper cuts off these offenders. If the end of an oar has been used unprotected, softwood grain will open almost like the bristles of a brush. Nothing much can be done, except sacrifice maybe 1 cm of end and clean off at the new length.

Common varnish is not fully waterproof, but it is sufficiently so for the intermittent use in water that an oar gets. Two-pot varnish is not usually advisable as the finish obtained may be fully waterproof but it is also hard and brittle, which does not suit the flexing of an oar. Rub down any remaining gloss of old varnish, touch up bare patches, and re-varnish all but the grip of the oar.

It is unwise to leave the end of a

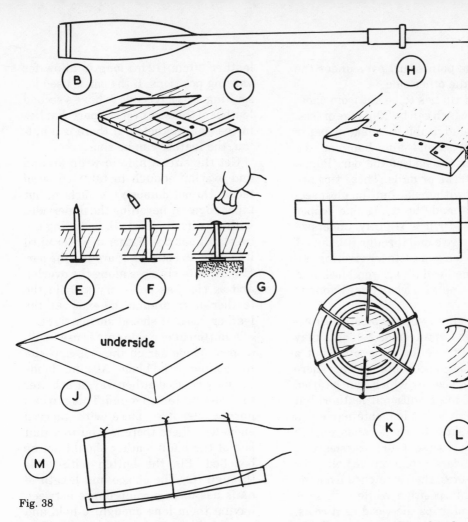

Fig. 38

wooden oar unprotected. At one time it was always coppered. Alternatives today are strips of plastic or sheathing with glassfibre and resin. An alternative to copper is a sea-water-resistant aluminium alloy. In a repair a metal band is preferable to plastic. Simplest is a band a short distance back from the end (B). Although the end may still sustain damage, wood is a kinder material than metal if it pushes against a boat, particularly an inflatable one. The metal strip is cut long enough for the ends to overlap. Holes are made by punches with a spike, then copper tacks used while the oar is resting on an iron block (C). Ideally, the tacks should be just long enough to go through the wood so that the points curl over under the metal on the other side.

A metal tip has to be cut from sheet material, which can be 20-gauge or less. It may be advisable to make a paper pattern (D). Bend and hammer the metal over the end of the oar. Punch holes for tacks or nails. These tips are often held with tacks, but the most secure end is made by using fine copper boat nails. Drill a slightly undersize hole and drive a nail through (E). Cut off the end to leave a little for riveting (F). Support the head on an iron block and spread the end with a ball pane hammer (G).

An oar suffers where it meets the rowlock if it is unprotected. Ash oars may stand up to this for some time, but a softwood oar needs protection. There are plastic sleeves which can be used instead of the traditional leather, but they are only suitable if obtainable in a matching size. Much depends on the plastic, but with some of these sleeves a slightly undersize one can be boiled for a few minutes, then stretched over the oar and into position while soft, so it shrinks and grips the wood as it cools. Otherwise, a sleeve that is an uncertain fit may need a few tacks.

The traditional protection, and still the most durable, is leather. A piece of hide is wrapped around the oar and tacked in place. There may be a button (H) to locate the oar in the rowlock, either one side or all round. If there is no button, it is advisable to have the leather 30 cm (12 in) long to allow for varying positions. If the oar is used for sculling, it is advisable to have a second leather of this size over the part that lies in the sculling notch. If there is a button, the leather can be shorter.

Get the size of hide to wrap around and overlap enough to take a row of tacks. Do not damage the surface, but taper edges by bevelling the undersides with a knife or chisel (J), including the overlap. Soak the leather in water until it is limp and stretch it around the oar. Use tacks fairly close along the overlap and as close as necessary to hold the leather down around the ends. As the leather dries, it should shrink tight.

A button at one side only is used with a spoon-blade oar on the side opposite the hollow of the blade. As a flat-blade oar may be used either way, it is better to have a button all round. This can be a narrow straplike piece with tapered ends (K). Where there is a button, that end of the main leather should not be bevelled. Fix the button with nails through (L). The choice and length of nails has to be a compromise between having them long enough to hold and not so large and plentiful as to weaken the wood at this point of great strain.

Frequent damage to an oar is a split in the blade. If this is clean and no parts have broken or splintered away, a synthetic resin glue can be used as soon as possible and the joint held together with adhesive tape while the glue sets. If a piece actually breaks away from an edge, the raggedness should be planed straight and a new piece of similar wood glued on. Allow for forming this piece after fitting, but do not make it any bigger than necessary to allow shaping. It can be held with string or tape (M) until the glue sets. Shaping can be done with a Surform tool, spokeshave or even a knife.

There is an advantage in being able to identify your oars quickly, particularly if they are kept with many others. It is worthwhile having your personal marking on the blade, preferably both sides, but this is best painted on when the wood has been rubbed down and before revarnishing, so the varnish protects the paint.

see also PADDLES.

Outboard motor problems

If a motor that has previously run properly produces problems, either in difficulty in starting, erratic running or misfiring, the trouble is almost certainly due to an easily-traced cause. Check that the approved drill has been observed and all the usual things attended to before suspecting something deeper and more in need of dismantling or expert attention. Of course, there may be a major fault, but a systematic check of the more superficial things will reveal the cause of the trouble in most cases. Providing the motor gets a supply of fuel in the correct mixture and a spark at the right time, it should run.

If the motor fails to start:
1. Check the fuel supply. See that the air vent screw is open, any taps in the fuel line are on and the hand pump, if there is one, is operable. See that fuel connections are correctly made and tight. Check that the carburettor has filled. Is the choke working?
2. Check the spark plugs. See that there is a spark. If a plug is fouled, clean it or replace it. If there is no spark, check the ignition wires and their insulation. See that all electrical connections are tight, clean and secure. If these are in order, check the coil and distributor. If there is battery ignition as well as electric starting, try using hand starting, so a partly-exhausted battery may only have to provide a spark. Re-charge the battery.
3. If the carburettor floods, check the float for leaks, or adjust the fuel level. If there has been an excess of fuel, leave the motor for ten minutes and try again, or remove the plugs and turn the engine over to blow out excess fuel before trying again.

Motor starts, then stops or misfires:
1. Check that the air vent in the fuel tank is open. Look for water in the fuel line. Suspect an incorrect fuel/oil mixture. Is the choke still set? Is the fuel level correct in the carburettor? A fuel

filter may be choked to the stage where it will not pass enough through. There may be a loose connection in the fuel lines so air is entering.

2. Check the plugs, one of which may be fouling intermittently. Check that magneto and distributor are working correctly.

3. See if the insulation, particularly around the ignition wiring, is sound and dry.

4. The motor may be overheating. Check that cooling water is circulating.

Misfiring:

1. Look for something moving or loose, that is only functioning occasionally.

2. Check that the mixture is not over-rich (choke still set?), particularly at low speeds.

3. Examine switches and terminals for dirt and wear, as well as clean close contact. See that the timing gear is not slipping.

4. Check for obstructions or water in the fuel system. Drain and wash out with petrol.

see also OUTBOARD MOTOR SECURITY; OUTBOARD MOTORS.

Outboard motor security (Fig. 39)

When an outboard motor is driving, the thrust is forward on the bottom of the transom and the load at the clamp position is twisting the top edge of the transom outwards (A). Even the best motor produces vibration and the clamp screws come under considerable strain. If the top edge of the transom is thickened as much as the clamps can span (B) right across to the gunwales, vibration is reduced and the risk of damage to the transom is minimized.

An alternative to the clamp screws is to bolt the mounting bracket to the transom. There should then be no risk of the motor jumping off. Some mounting brackets have slots to fit over bolts in addition to the clamp screws. These provide additional safety, but allow the motor to be removed without loosening bolts. They also ensure the motor being replaced at the same spot each time.

A device that fits across the clamp screw heads and can be locked discourages theft and prevents the screws vibrating loose. Using a pad, either plastic or home-made of wood (C), locates the clamp screw ends and prevents slightly loosened screws allowing the motor to jump off.

Many motors have an anchorage for a safety chain. Ideally, this should be as short as possible and arranged directly downwards so a loosening clamp cannot lift high enough to come away from the transom (D). It may be possible to include a padlock in this chain to discourage theft. If there is no anchorage on the motor it may be possible to take a chain or wire cable around the motor to a secure point in the boat. The pull of a motor jumping off may be considerable,

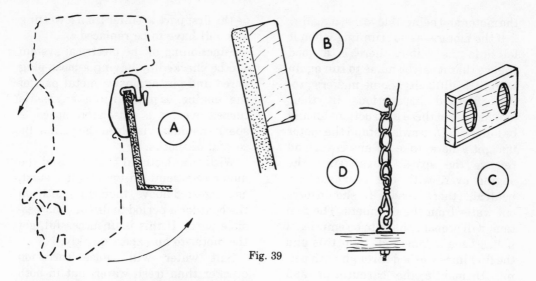

Fig. 39

so fibre rope and wood screws at the attachment point should not be used.

If a motor is light enough to lift off, it should be removed when the boat is out of use or is being trailed. If the motor has to remain on the transom when the boat is afloat and unattended, a strong chain around it and a padlock to a secure anchor point in the boat is advisable to supplement any other locking device. If the motor is to remain on the transom when trailing, check that any strut arrangement is adequate to withstand vibration and road shocks if the motor is to travel tilted. If the propeller projects it should be covered by a stout bag or in some other way to protect it and anything coming into contact with it, as well as to comply with the law.

see also OUTBOARD MOTOR, SUB- MERGED; OUTBOARD MOTORS.

Outboard motor, submerged

If an outboard motor is dropped in the water, its treatment will depend on whether it was running or not at the time and how long it was submerged. If the motor was running, it is very likely that something will be bent or broken. In this case, the only hope of putting the motor back into service is to return it to the manufacturer or an approved agent. Some makers ask that all you do is drain off as much water as possible and return the motor to them. Obviously this should be done quickly as it may mean the difference between scrapping the motor and being able to use it again.

If the motor was not running when it fell into the water, there is a good chance that it can be made to run again with little difficulty. Some makers provide first-aid instructions in their handbook and these instructions should be followed. Otherwise, stand the motor upright ashore, take off any cover and remove the spark plugs. Turn the engine over, with the gear shift in neutral, if there is one. This should force out water from the cylinders. The fuel tank will probably have to be emptied if it has been submerged, then this and the fuel lines washed through with petrol. Dismantle the carburettor and clean out any moisture, then wash thoroughly with petrol.

Re-assemble the parts and hold the motor upright and rigid while a start is tried. If it starts, stop it immediately. Mount it on the boat and run it at a moderate speed for about thirty minutes. This should dry-out parts out of reach.

If it will not start, this is probably because the electrical system is too wet to function. The trouble may only be moisture on the plugs. If possible change the plugs, otherwise dry them, preferably with hot air, then wipe oil around the plug holes and replace them. Open the distributor, probably by removing a plate on the flywheel, and dry it, also with warm air if possible. A silicone-grease spray for counteracting moisture may be used. A condenser may

be the first part to suffer from a wetting and will have to be replaced.

Functioning of the electrical system can be checked by having a loose plug wired and put against a metal part of the engine casing. If the engine is turned over at a reasonable speed, a spark should be visible at the points. Be careful of shocks.

With the electrical gear dry and the motor re-assembled try another start, as suggested above, then run gently on the boat for a period to dry out inaccessible parts. If this is unsuccessful, get the motor to an expert quickly.

Salt water will cause corrosion quicker than fresh water, but in both cases it is after the motor has been removed from the water that corrosion starts. Water alone does not corrode much; it is a combination of water and air that does the damage. Fresh water can be used to remove salt water, but methylated spirits (alcohol) can be used to rinse away water. The water/spirit combination will evaporate, but affected surfaces should be coated with oil, if possible. Even when a recovered motor has been made to run again, it is advisable to follow with a better than usual service as soon as possible, as there may be moisture trapped that will cause corrosion to continue and progressively affect the performance of the motor.

see also OUTBOARD MOTOR SECURITY; OUTBOARD MOTORS.

Outboard motors

Nearly all outboard motors are two-stroke. If a four-stroke outboard motor has to be serviced, these notes should be read in conjunction with the notes on inboard motors, most of which are four-stroke. A two-stroke motor is simple, but it runs most efficiently at high speeds, which will be reduced by gearing to the propeller. Lubrication of most parts comes from oil mixed with the fuel.

With some motors the choice of fuel grade and the right proportion of the specified grade of oil (not usually multi-grade) is critical to satisfactory performance. These should be mixed thoroughly. For some motors, particularly those with an integral tank, the makers advise mixing petrol and oil in a can first. With a separate tank it is usually sufficient to have some fuel in the tank, then add the right amount of oil, followed by the rest of the fuel. Use a can with a nozzle if possible. If a funnel is used, it should have a filter and not be used for any other purpose. Any petrol/oil mixture spilled or left on a surface will eventually leave a film of oil after the petrol has evaporated. This may happen in a carburettor, if left full and the motor has not been used for some time, resulting in there being too much oil in the first mixture to get through to the cylinders when an attempt is made to restart, with possible oiling of plugs. If an engine will be unused for some time, turn off petrol and let the engine run until fuel starvation stops it, then the carburettor will have emptied. Alternatively, if there is a drain plug, empty the carburettor bowl.

Cleanliness in the fuel system is important. It is unwise to leave fuel in the tank when the motor is out of use for long periods. At the end of the season, drain the tank – it can be used in the car. There are one or more filters in the fuel system. How often they need cleaning depends on what is found on inspection, but during annual servicing, at least, they should be dismantled and washed out with methylated spirit or petrol. They may stop water as well as solid impurities. Allow some fuel to run to waste from the fuel lines before reconnecting filters, to ensure trapped water is released.

Besides fuel, the motor requires a good spark in each cylinder at the right time. This is the sole purpose of the electrical system on most motors and the spark plug is the vital piece of equipment that delivers the spark. It is important to follow the maker's recommendations. Some motors will not function or may perform indifferently when fitted with a perfectly good, but wrong, plug. Examine plugs occasionally. If the engine is functioning properly, wire brushing to clean the points may be all that is needed. Check the gap with a feeler gauge and correct this by bending the outer arm, if necessary.

Wire brushing, removing accumulated matter by hand and adjusting by bending a point are really emergency on-the-spot treatments. It is better to let a garage clean the plugs with their specialized equipment. Because of this it is worthwhile having a set of extra plugs, known to be in good condition, to use as replacements, rather than try to service a plug afloat. A much-used outboard motor will benefit from a change to new plugs more often than is frequently done.

The fact that a spark is occurring can be checked by having the plug loose with the wire connected, then holding it by its insulation (to avoid shock) so its metal body is in close contact with a metal part of the engine. Turn over the engine and you should be able to see a spark between the points.

Electricity to produce a spark may come from a magneto or through a coil or other means from a battery. Timing of the spark(s) is controlled by a distributor, reached on many engines by removing a cover on the flywheel, but check what to do in the maker's handbook. Wear may occur between the points, which become pitted and uneven. They can be filed level and will then need adjusting to the gap specified in the handbook. If the points are badly worn, it is better to replace them.

The parts of the electrical system depend for proper functioning on heavy wire, proper insulation and tight connections. Doubtful cables should be replaced. Clean meeting surfaces bright by scraping or rubbing with abrasive. See that any metal fittings on the ends of cables are secure and there is a clean contact with the wire, preferably soldered. Make sure any particles of metal produced in cleaning surfaces are removed, otherwise there may be leakage of current. Modern plastic used in electrical gear is very tough, but a damaged case or other part may have a crack, not immediately apparent, that will trap moisture and provide a path for current to leak. Connections, cables and electrical parts should be sprayed with a moisture-resistant non-conductive sealer. If such a sealer has already been used and electrical gear is dismantled for servicing and reassembled, make sure none of the old sprayed sealer comes between parts that should make a good contact.

If an outboard motor has been functioning without problems, servicing the fuel system and electrical gear is all that need be undertaken at the engine as routine attention. It is unwise to open cylinders or other enclosed parts of the engine, unless trouble there is suspected, and if this is so, it may be better to let an expert handle it.

Drive to the propeller is via a shaft to a gearbox forward of the propeller. There may be a clutch and water pump as well. With most motors a jet of water escaping from a hole is used as an indicator that water is circulating. If this stops and does not soon start again, the engine should be stopped, otherwise it will be damaged by overheating. It is unusual for the water pump to develop a fault and it may be that the water intake is blocked. This may free itself if the engine is stopped. Otherwise, and during routine servicing, clean the spaces in the grill or holes of the water intake. Be careful to poke debris out and not push it in.

The gears in the lower unit are working in grease or oil. The method of refilling or topping-up is described in the handbook. In many motors the grease is available in a tube. This is applied in one hole in the casing, after removing a plug, and grease squeezed in until grease uncontaminated with water is seen to emerge from another hole, then the plugs are screwed in. In another type an oil has to be poured in to a specified level.

Apart from anything else in servicing an outboard motor, check every connection for security. Even in the best engines there is vibration, and loose connections soon become looser. Be careful of washers, particularly in a place like the lower casing, where they are necessary for oil and water proofing. If no other locking arrangements are used on a nut, it can be prevented from loosening by one of the glue-like mixtures available in a tube to squeeze on. If a nut is secured by a split pin (cotter pin), it is not considered good engineering practice to use the same pin again as it may break where it has been straigh-

tened and rebent. If it has to be used again, try to get the bends in different places. Hose and pipe clips may loosen or they may break through the pipe they are around. A leak inwards may be as much a problem as one outwards. Air entering a fuel or water system may cause malfunctioning.

Check the mounting, tilting and fixing arrangements. Moving parts should be cleaned and lightly greased. Light alloy parts are best dismantled and any corrosion (white powder) removed, then re-assembled with graphite grease. Some tilt arrangements include friction washers. Check that these are sound. There may have to be new washers or adjustment for wear.

If the motor tiller includes a twist-grip throttle, grease the moving parts in the tiller and follow through into the motor cowling to grease other parts of the linkage. Any exposed parts of the gear-change mechanism should be similarly lubricated. Aim to get enough grease between parts that move over each other, but wipe off any surplus. Keep grease away from electrical gear. If reverse is by turning the complete motor the mounting may include a grease nipple, which should receive attention, otherwise slide the joint apart so surfaces can be greased. It should be possible to turn the motor completely round without uneven movement due to dirt or bare metal being apparent.

At least once a year clean off the

exterior of a motor. It can be wiped with a degreasing fluid or a cleaning solvent. Most motors are made of salt-water-resistant materials, so corrosion should be no problem, but for the sake of appearances damaged paintwork may be touched up. Although internal parts may not corrode, a build-up of salt in the waterways could cause trouble and running the motor in fresh water whenever possible is advisable. If the boat cannot be taken on to fresh water, the motor may be mounted via a rigidly-fixed board so its lower part is immersed in a drum of water, then run long enough to get warm and the waterways thoroughly flushed out.

The exhaust system of more advanced motors is internal and unlikely to go wrong or need servicing. Some small motors have an external silencer and exhaust which may corrode, so a replacement is necessary. Little can be done once corrosion has become advanced. In some motors the exhaust gases pass out through the propeller centre. These motors have a slip arrangement on the propeller to take care of underwater obstructions, but if the motor uses a shear pin or a spring (e.g. British Seagull), routine servicing should include examination of these things, as they may partly shear and continue to function, but may finally fail without warning if not replaced.

see also INBOARD ENGINES, PETROL; INBOARD PETROL ENGINE FAULTS; OUT-BOARD MOTOR PROBLEMS; OUTBOARD MOTOR SECURITY; OUTBOARD MOTOR, SUBMERGED; PROPELLER.

Outdrive (inboard/outboard or Z drive)

An outdrive is a finely-engineered piece of equipment that should get as much servicing as the engine which drives it. However, it is unwise to do more than superficial inspecting and maintenance without a maker's handbook. There should be regular visual checks, but annually, or at intervals specified by the makers, the drive should be stripped and serviced, either professionally or by the owner with the aid of a handbook.

Oil level should be checked regularly. The drive should not use oil. If the level appears to increase, this may be because of water getting in, as evidenced by a soupy mixture. Too much oil could cause oil to reach the clutch and affect it. Water might enter because of a faulty washer around the dipstick, and this should be replaced. If there is any doubt about the oil, and in any case at the annual inspection, drain the old oil and refill.

There are synthetic rubber bellows that should be inspected for wear, particularly at parts that may rub when the outdrive is raised. The bellows over the drive shaft is the important one. This and the water intake bellows should be intact, but an exhaust bellows may be made with a drainage hole to release water.

Also check any hoses visible. Any replacement hose clip should be stainless steel and in some outdrives it is necessary to position the projecting part of a clip in the right place to avoid fouling when the outdrive moves. See that hoses and bellows have adequate overlap and clips compress them at the right points. Note the arrangement on old parts before replacing. Hot water may soften synthetic rubber if cold conditions make it difficult to stretch or press into place.

Remove debris, particularly from moving parts. Check water intakes, which may be holes or a grill. Be careful to poke out anything lodged there, rather than push it in.

Examine the propeller and its associated equipment. It will be advisable to remove it occasionally and look for fishing line that may be wound around the shaft and find its way into bearings. There may be a sacrificial anode in or near the assembly. This protects other metal parts from electrolytic action and is intended to be eaten away. If it is badly affected, replace it.

If the outer unit is to be removed from the backplate on the transom, the handbook will describe the method, but remember that the assembly that comes away is quite heavy. Apart from the problem of taking the weight as it comes away, studs, bolt ends and other connections could be damaged by careless handling. Wedges and chocks under the skeg will take the weight and allow tilting to clear attachments, but have a helper to control the unit as it is removed.

Paddles

Paddles may be used for moving a sailing dinghy on placid waters when there is no wind, or they may be provided for use with a liferaft. There is a tendency to regard them as of no consequence, until they are needed and found wanting.

For all-wood paddles maintenance is similar to oars. Many paddles have plastic blades. Some of the plastic used tends to crack with age. Nothing much can be done about this. For many of the plastics used there is no adhesive. It may be possible to bind with self-adhesive tape. Some plastics will melt with heat. Try a hot soldering bit on an unimportant part to see if it melts. Cut shavings from another part, then use the soldering bit along a crack while feeding on the shavings, like solder, to melt new material into the crack and run the edges together.

Some plastic blades are sleeved over a wooden shaft. Breaks there or loosening may be taken care of by more screws in sound parts. A very loose shaft may be withdrawn and bound with tape before inserting.

Another type of paddle uses an aluminium alloy tube as a shaft and this may be coated with plastic. The blade is wood and plugged into the end of the tube. If a blade breaks, leaving the plug in the tube, remove any retaining screw, then drive a stout screw into the end of the broken plug, like a corkscrew, and grip this in a vice to pull the plug out. If this is unsuccessful drill a hole of at least half the diameter of the plug right through its centre. It should then be possible to break away the remaining wood with a narrow chisel. Some paddle suppliers offer stock replacement blades, otherwise one can be made with a piece of plywood and strips each side to make up the thickness to shape a round plug. This plug and any handle at the other end should fit tightly so the tube is watertight and will float.

It is sometimes possible to make a broken oar into a paddle. While this is a good way of salvaging something that would otherwise be scrapped, make it comfortable to handle. The top should be well rounded. It may be necessary to thin down or reshape the neck for the lower hand to grip. Some larger oars have blades much too long for paddles and may benefit from cutting off. A paddle can be a difficult and tiring thing to use if much progress is to be made in a dinghy or other boat, so the paddle should be finished well, then it cannot be blamed for the user's inefficiency. Examine a canoe paddle and see how strength in the right places is coupled with lightness.

see also OARS.

Paint

Conditions afloat, particularly in salt water, can be hard on paint and it is false economy to use anything except paint intended for boats. There may be little to choose between the best household exterior paint and marine paint for some purposes, but it is advisable to only use the products of a manufacturer specializing in marine paints. All of the manufacturers of these paints provide brochures and other instructions, which should be studied before choosing paint and starting work. It is then advisable to use one paint system, employing the products of one manufacturer.

Traditional paints were made with natural pigments in oil, plus other things to give special features and hasten drying. Although some oil paints of this form may still be made, for most purposes afloat it is better to choose a modern synthetic paint, which should last longer, retain better protection and appearance and be quicker drying. Reasonably quick drying to a dust-free stage is valuable in reducing the period when the surface can become marred by flying dirt and insects. Although tradi-

tional paints were applied to protect wood, they were not waterproof. Not all synthetic paints are waterproof, but they do give better protection. Many of them dry harder so they have a better resistance to abrasion.

Several attractive and much-advertised paints are suitable for household purposes, and are unsuitable for boats. Many of the specialized marine paints are described as polyurethane. If they are one-can types, they can be treated as ordinary paint and may be expected to have about the same life.

The toughest marine paints are in two cans, which have to be mixed before use. As the chemical setting process commences when the parts are mixed, there must be no delay in application, although the setting time allows the work to be done without undue haste. There are two-can polyurethane and epoxy paints. Their final surface is very hard and waterproof. There may be little elasticity so there is a risk of cracking or breaking away if used over a surface that moves.

At one time there were several types of paint for different marine applications, but modern synthetics have more universal uses. In some paint systems there is a primer for use as a first coat. This is compounded to penetrate the surface, if it is porous like wood, and provide a grip that will retain subsequent coats. The colour of the primer does not have to match the further coats. Different primers may be specified for different base materials. Primer, if needed, is followed by one or more undercoats. These are matt when they dry and in a colour the same as or complementary to the top coat. It is the satisfactory base built up by the undercoats, as much as the quality of the top coat, that decides the effectiveness of the final appearance. The top coat, usually gloss, is what is seen and has to take wear and exposure.

In the systems of some makers there is no primer and one paint may be used for all coats. In traditional paints, gloss was not put over gloss without the lower coat being rubbed down with abrasive, but some synthetics will make a good bond with an earlier coat providing they are applied within a certain time. If there has to be a delay, the lower coat will have to have its gloss rubbed off.

Household primer is not good enough for wood in boats. The usual marine type is metallic. For steel there are primers with rust-inhibiting properties. For non-ferrous metals including galvanized steel, there is a zinc chromate primer. For new bright metal there are primers which get a grip by the use of phosphoric acid. If later coats are to be two-can types, the primer on any surface should be a two-can type. This can be followed with one-can conventional paints, but the one-can primer is unsatisfactory under two-can paint.

Undercoats should match the top coats and the makers' recommendations should be followed.

Nearly all top coats have a gloss finish. This looks smarter and is easier to keep clean than a matt or semi-gloss surface, but paints with less than a full gloss can be had. The word 'enamel' in this context means a gloss paint. Some single-can paints may be described as polyurethane or acrylic, indicating their special make-up, but they are treated as conventional paints.

Twin-pack polyurethane paint is obtainable in the usual colours. Not such a large range of colours may be obtainable in twin-pack epoxy paint.

Deck paints have only a partial gloss and may contain something to give a safe foothold. Sand in conventional paint is used, but the makers may claim ingredients of special quality. There are bilge paints suitable for hidden places. Aluminium paint is used to brighten worn galvanizing and may be heat-resistant for use on engine parts. A condensation-resistant paint may contain granulated cork. Other paints are made for water and fuel tanks.

Paint is supplied in containers of many sizes. Although larger quantities may be proportionately more economical, it is unwise to keep paint for long in a partly-full can. It should be transferred to a smaller container, with minimum air space. For most purposes it is probably wiser to only buy the amount needed immediately and use the complete contents of a can. Some two-part finishes have limited shelf life, so check the limiting date.

see *also* ANTI-FOULING; BOOT-TOPPING; DECKS; FOOT RAILS; PAINTING TOOLS; PAINTING AND VARNISHING; PAINT STRIPPING; SOLVENTS; STOPPINGS; VARNISH.

Paint stripping

If paint or varnish has reached a stage where it would be wiser to remove it and start again than to attempt to patch it and paint over, it can be removed by one of several methods: by mechanical means, such as scraping or sanding; by a chemical stripper; or by burning it off.

Which method to use depends on the base material as well as the type of finish to be removed. Burning off is suitable for paint on wood, but should not be used for varnish as the inevitable char marks will show through if the new coat is also to be varnish. A paraffin or other liquid fuel blowlamp can be used, but bottled gas is more convenient. A portable lamp with a disposable gas cartridge is convenient as it can be taken anywhere, but it is much more expensive to use than a lamp fed by a pipe from a larger container.

Although almost any flame will soften paint, a nozzle that gives a broad flat flame is best. Use a stripping knife or scraper. The stripping knife is for broad surfaces and has a wide edge to push under and lift the paint. It is not intended to cut. For narrow places it may be possible to use a filling or putty knife, but it is more usual to change to a shave hook or scraper. This is used with a pull action. The basic tool is triangular, but a multi-edged type is needed for mouldings and other curves. The edge is maintained by filing. Although not intended to have a cutting edge like a wood scraper, the edge should be more knifelike than the push-action stripping knife.

Use a flame with a swinging action at a distance that will be found to soften the paint film without burning the wood. This depends on the intensity of the flame, but be careful not to get too close or dwell on one spot. It is the outer part of the flame that is hot, not the blue cone at the centre. Deal with a small area at a time and scrape with one hand, while swinging the flame with the other hand. Dealing with broad areas is soon mastered, but be careful at corners or high parts of mouldings, where careless use of the flame can char the projecting angles. Of course, once wood has been charred and burned, nothing can be done to revive it and it has to be scraped or sanded down to a sound surface. On vertical surfaces it is usual to work from the bottom upwards. In some places it is better to work along the lines of grain or in the long direction of a panel. The scraper should be removing paint only and not a film of wood. Stoppings used under paint are not usually affected by the flame if no more heat than is required to lift the paint is used.

Some chemical paint strippers can be used on paint or varnish on any base material. Although a flame might be used on metal it should not be brought near glassfibre, where heat would spoil the surface at least and might set the material on fire. If there have been glassfibre repairs to a wood hull, do not use a flame to remove paint over the repair. Read the instructions accompanying a chemical paint stripper, and if it is not specifically quoted as suitable for glassfibre, it is better to rely on mechanical abrasion only for cleaning off old paint.

Most paint strippers are quite potent. They have to be to do the job. Consequently, protect the hands, wear old clothes and be careful the liquid does not get on upholstery or surfaces not intended to be stripped. Have the recommended neutralizer available for use in case of accident. Some strippers are inflammable, so work in a well ventilated place, avoid naked flames and do not smoke. Some give off dangerous fumes, particularly if they meet burning tobacco.

A chemical paint stripper is an alternative to a flame. Apply it with a brush. The paint will blister and come away, ready to be removed with a scraper. Most strippers will also remove varnish and leave a surface ready for new varnish. One danger is the stripper soaking into stoppings, which it may soften and remove. Neutralize particularly thoroughly around stoppings, otherwise retained stripper may leach to the surface and spoil any new coat of varnish.

Not all strippers are neutralized in the same way, so follow the maker's instructions and leave a surface the recommended time before applying fresh paint or varnish. Be careful when disposing of the removed paint and stripper mixture. It is unwise to leave it to be walked on. If it is burned, do this in the open and avoid breathing the resulting fumes.

Mechanical removal of paint can be done with abrasive cloth or paper. Hand methods are slow, but with the material wrapped around a block there is little risk of damage to the underlying surface and the treatment should improve the surface, eliminating the sanding which quite often has to follow stripping with a flame or chemical. A power sander is much quicker, but can be difficult to control. A disc sander leaves curved marks which may be hidden under paint, but would not be acceptable under varnish. A belt sander puts the scratches in line, so marks are disguised if taken in the direction of grain on wood.

Care is needed with either type of mechanical sander to avoid digging in at the edge of the abrasive surface. There is also the difficulty of removing the paint or varnish, but not taking away too much of the underlying surface. Because of the hardness of metal, this loss will be minimal; but on wood careless power sanding may leave a marred surface needing much hard work to put right, while on glassfibre the gel coat is quite thin and this should not be broken through to expose glass filaments, which will soak up water by capillary action.

Besides the use of abrasive it is possible to use a scraper without flame or chemical to remove paint or varnish from wood. This should be a wood scraper; the most convenient one is the hook type with replaceable blades, such as the Skarsten. This is used with a firm pressure so the cut is right through the paint film and actually removes a very thin sliver of wood from the surface. This may be combined with abrasive, but a sharp scraper on mahogany, teak or other quality boatbuilding wood should leave a surface that needs little preparation for a new coat of varnish.

see also PAINT; PAINTING TOOLS; PAINTING AND VARNISHING; STOPPINGS; VARNISH.

Painting and varnishing

Most paint maintenance is done by brushing, and this is generally advisable. A roller can be used on a large clear area, but spraying is best left to the professional.

A satisfactory finish starts with the preparation of the base surface. Bare wood should be sanded with progressively finer abrasives, but not so fine as to produce a polished surface. It may help to moisten the surface after early sanding. This will raise minute fibres that have turned over and they can be sanded off. Glassfibre to be painted should be wiped over with a solvent to remove traces of parting agent or wax polish. Some paint manufacturers supply an oil-removing fluid for this purpose. It should also be used on oily wood, such as teak, just before painting or varnishing. Petrol or a clothes-cleaning fluid can be used. Any gloss on glassfibre should be removed with fine abrasive, which could be sheet or a scouring powder. Steel to be painted should have rust removed mechanically and may be treated with a rust-inhibiting fluid before painting, but follow the instructions of the paint maker.

If the old surface is good, it should be cleaned. Salt should be washed off as particles of salt remaining will affect the paint finish. Sugar soap may be bought for paint cleaning, or a detergent can be used, but whatever is used should be washed off with plenty of fresh water, then allowed to dry. Flakes of loose paint should be removed and the whole surface sanded, particularly if there is any remaining gloss of the old paint.

Types of paint are described in the section on 'Paint'. Application generally is similar, except that some synthetic paints and varnishes should not be brushed out any more than is absolutely necessary. Other paints may benefit from a good working out over the surface with each brushful, but if the instructions are to avoid brushing out, it is necessary to flow on the paint and do no more brushing than is necessary to spread the paint and leave it so it will not run. Some practice on a less important part is advisable.

Fortunately modern marine paints dry to a dust-free state fairly quickly, but to avoid damage by dust, wipe fluff and dust from the surface with a fluffless cloth (an old and much washed rag) lightly moistened with white spirit, or with a bought tack rag. Do not wear fluffy clothing. If the work has to be done in a place where sawdust and shavings have been produced, these should have been removed some time before painting commences. If it is an area that can be sprayed with water, that will help to prevent the spread of dust. If an insect pitches on wet paint, leave it. Pulling off after the paint has dried will only leave a very minute mark.

Paint strokes should usually follow the long way of the panel being painted. However, if strokes can be up and down on a surface approaching vertical, there is less risk of runs or curtains, where an excess of paint runs to make a hanging thick blob, which can only be removed by sanding and painting over if it occurs too late to be brushed out.

If there are two different colours adjoining, it is usually best to do the lighter colour first, as any that goes over the line is more easily covered by the darker colour. Masking tape avoids this trouble. It is usual to paint or varnish higher parts before lower parts, because of the risk of damaging a lower finished surface.

Modern finishes are not so easily affected by weather conditions as traditional paints made from natural ingredients, but results will still be better in the right conditions. Paint and varnish thicken at low temperatures. Store and use them in reasonable temperatures – about 18°C (68°F) is ideal. Varnish, in particular, benefits from standing the container in warm water for a period before use, if air temperatures are low. Do not heat excessively and avoid applying on a very hot day, if possible.

An excess of moisture in the air will affect paint. It is obviously wrong to apply paint while it is raining, but a very humid atmosphere will also spoil a paint finish. Winds may cause uneven drying and a patchy appearance, as well as bringing dust to mar the surface.

Dip only about half of the bristles into the paint and wipe off excess, then spread the paint on the wood. Primer and undercoat should be brushed out by working in several directions, to achieve a good spread and maximum penetration if it is a porous surface. This also reduces the risk of there being an excess of paint anywhere that may settle as runs.

If the top coat is a type that can be brushed out, it can also be spread in this way, but final strokes should be the long way and taken towards the area covered by the previous brushing. With most paints brush marks flow out and do not show in the finished work, but by taking the last strokes of a particular application back towards the previously painted area and lifting the brush as it crosses the older paint, there can be little risk of brush marks or blemishes remaining on the finished work. If it is a type of paint that should not be worked out, the brush strokes will have to be nearly all in the final direction, but it is important to finish by lifting the brush over the previously painted surface.

Working in this way gives a good finish, but there may be a problem when covering a large area with paint that dries fairly quickly, as an earlier part may have dried so it is already hardening when a new brushful is finished over it. This will not blend as smoothly. For this sort of work it is necessary to scheme the coverage so no edge is left too long awaiting the adjoining paint, or it may be better to use a paint that does not dry as quickly. The drying time of most paints is affected by temperature and circulation of air. Cold conditions and a closed room will slow setting.

Faults in painting are usually due to the condition of the surface below the paint film. Paint is unlikely to blister due to anything within itself unless heated much higher than any normal conditions would produce. Moisture in the surface below may cause blisters. Sometimes oil or resin in the wood comes to the surface and paint blisters over it. Blistering on steel may be due to rust forming below the paint.

Paint may flake or peel over a damp or greasy surface. It could happen if the wood or metal surface has been excessively smoothed to the point of being polished. If a hard paint is put over a soft one, the under layer may creep, then the surface crocodiles and becomes patterned. Using the wrong or no primer may cause paint to come away. The weather can cause some paints to become chalky. The dust produced may run and disfigure varnish-work lower down. There is no cure, other than repainting.

Paint may set without a gloss or with a patchy gloss if it is affected by rain, dew or frost. It is always advisable to paint and varnish early in the day, so the surface is dry long before nightfall.

Although paints are now manufactured to rigid formulae and colours should be consistent, it is safest to obtain all the paint of one colour needed for a job at one time. If there is any mixing, enough should be prepared for the whole job. This also applies if the paint is thinned. Thinned and unthinned paint may dry to a slightly different shade, so all should be the same consistency.

With traditional paints made from natural materials it was usual to leave each coat any convenient time before applying another coat. With many of the synthetic paints the makers specify minimum and maximum times during which another coat should be applied. This is important to get the maximum bond between coats. If there has to be a long delay, it may be sufficient to rub down the fully hardened coat and then proceed; some makers require a special intermediate coat to be introduced before the next coat. To get the best result from modern paints it is important to study the system and arrange the timing and conditions of your painting to conform as far as possible. Fortunately, the makers of marine paints provide plenty of instructions for use of their products.

see also PAINT; PAINT STRIPPING; PAINTING TOOLS; SOLVENTS; STOPPINGS; VARNISH.

Painting tools (Fig. 40)

The quality of a paint finish is affected by the quality of the brush. It is better to buy a good brush and care for it than to buy a cheap brush and discard it. Even the best brush will shed hairs at first. An older brush will not give this trouble. Natural bristle is best, but expensive. The nearest synthetic to it is nylon. Some modern finishes are not compatible with some synthetic brushes, so check any makers' instructions.

Brushes vary in thickness as well as in width. A cheap thin brush will not carry much paint and will not leave such a good surface. The best brushes are often described as 'varnish' brushes. This does not mean they are only suitable for varnish, but that varnish requires a good brush, and they are equally suitable for paint. A large brush gives best results on a large surface, but 10 cm (4 in) is as large as most workers will want to handle. For smaller places there may be other sizes down to 1 cm (½ in).

Paint rollers have uses, but not as many as in household decorating. A roller is much quicker than a brush and should give a more even application. It tends to use more paint. It does not achieve as good a penetration on bare wood and a first coat on new or stripped wood should be by brush, even if subsequent coats are by roller.

Even quicker than rollers, in actual application, is spraying. Preparations, masking of other parts and cleaning afterwards may cancel any time gained in application, except when very large areas are involved. Paint for spraying has to be thinned, so more coats are needed.

A dusting brush is useful for cleaning ahead of painting. Any soft hand-sweeping brush can be used. Things

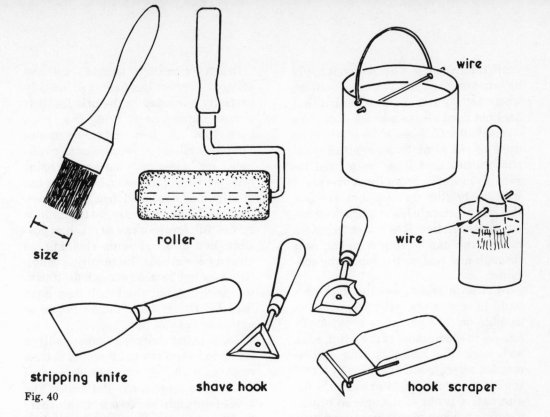

size

roller

wire

wire

stripping knife

shave hook

hook scraper

Fig. 40

may have to be improvised for such jobs as getting at the inside of a centreboard case, where cloth or felt wrapped over a strip of wood may be used instead of a brush.

Most people use paint direct from the can. If the paint has settled and needs mixing, this cannot be done with a full can so the contents should be transferred to a larger container. If there is much liquid above fairly thick settlement, pour off some of the liquid and mix what is left with a flat (not round) piece of wood, or with a mechanical stirrer, which may be a bent rod driven by

an electric drill. Progressively add the remaining liquid and stir it in.

For large jobs it is better to transfer the paint to another container, which may be a plastic or galvanized paint kettle. Wiping a brush on the side of a can soon leads to drips and may cause hardened paint inside which will affect the remaining paint. A wire across the centre of the can is a worthwhile addition, so wiping the brush on it returns surplus into the body of the paint.

A paint brush that is to be used again soon may be stored in water overnight. Water keeps air from the paint and prevents it hardening. This does not apply to brushes used for two-can finishes, where setting is a chemical action that does not need air, so a brush should be cleaned after this use, even if it is to be used for the same finish again. Do not put brushes that have been used for varnish in water. Store them overnight with the bristles immersed in varnish. It is bad practice to leave a brush standing on its bristles. It is better to have a hole in the handle so a wire can pass through and rest on the top of the container.

To clean a brush, use the back of a knife to scrape out as much paint as possible on to a pad of newspaper. To remove the remainder of the paint, soak and work the brush in the recommended solvent, which is usually white spirit for normal paints or varnish. An alternative is one of the special brush-cleaning fluids, which is more amenable to washing out with water afterwards. After this, wash the brush in warm water with soap or a synthetic detergent, then swill this away with clean water.

If a brush is not to be used again for some time, wrap the end in paper after it has dried. Fold this over the bristles so as to keep their shape. Even with very thorough cleaning there may be traces of paint left in a brush. This may not matter for further painting, but a brush that has been used for paint should not be used later for varnish, as it may contaminate and colour.

Brush cleaning should not be delayed. If paint has hardened, or only partially hardened in the bristles, it is almost impossible to bring the brush back into the best condition again. There are chemical preparations available for cleaning hardened paint brushes. One of these can be used or the bristles may be soaked in paint stripper. If softening and loosening of the paint is successful, scrape away as much as possible and proceed with cleaning as already described. The resulting condition may not be good enough for finishing painting, but the brush may have uses for rough work in the bilges or applying anti-fouling.

Some paint stripping is done with a flame to loosen the paint which is then removed with a stripping knife or paint scraper for large fairly flat areas. The blade is straight across the end and may be 10 cm (4 in) or less in width. It does not have a true cutting edge, but is thin enough to get under the loosened paint and remove it. In some narrower places a filling or putty knife with a square end may be used, but the tool for angles and mouldings is a shave hook, which may be triangular or multi-edged for curved sections. This is kept sharp by filing.

Paint may also be removed mechanically. There are abrasives to use by hand or power, or paint can be removed from wood with a wood scraper. It could be the flat cabinet type or a Skarsten hook type with replaceable blades.

Masking tape, which is a self-adhesive paper tape that does not leave any stickiness when peeled, has many uses in defining areas and ensuring firm, true lines. It can also hold sheets of paper over surrounding surfaces when preparing to spray. Masking tape should only be used over absolutely dry paint or varnish, otherwise some of the paint may lift. If masking tape is used to provide a true edge by letting the paint go over it, and the paint is a type that dries very hard, peel the tape off after the paint has set sufficiently, but before it has become fully hardened, when it might crack or fracture.

see also ABRASIVES; ANTI-FOULING; BOOT-TOPPING; PAINT; PAINT STRIPPING; PAINTING AND VARNISHING; SOLVENTS; VARNISH.

Personal buoyancy

There have been changes in knowledge and experience concerning garments and other devices to provide reserve personal buoyancy in recent years, and any lifejacket, buoyancy aid or other personal flotation gear of unknown age should be suspect. At one time kapok was used as a buoyant material. This vegetable material is buoyant, but it will absorb water and after about six hours can be so waterlogged as to be ineffective. In some aids the kapok is in sealed plastic cases so water cannot reach it, but as these are liable to puncture, such arrangements are not now considered acceptable.

Plastic foam is now used as a buoyant material. The modern type is closed-cell, in which the puncture of one cell does not allow water to transfer to another cell. This is the usual type of buoyant material in modern aids and it should give no trouble. During the transition stage from kapok to closed-cell plastic foam, there was a type of foam in which the cells were interconnected. This meant that water could be soaked up like a sponge, although good buoyancy was provided while the foam was in a watertight case. If there is doubt about plastic foam, trying its water absorption will show which type it is. If it absorbs water it should not be used, and either the foam should be replaced or the garment discarded. Cork, as a buoyant material, is no longer acceptable except for some lifebuoys.

In Britain, the term 'lifejacket' is only applied to an aid approved by the British Standards Institution, which conforms to certain conditions. Because of the requirement that the lifejacket should turn an unconscious person face up and support his face clear of the water, there has to be some bulk in front and this may be found to interfere with some activities. Because of this there is an alternative 'buoyancy aid', which will support a person in the water, but assumes he is conscious and able to take action to keep his head above water. Most buoyancy aids are approved by the Ship and Boat Builders National Federation. Foreign lifejackets or buoyancy aids do not carry British classifications, but they may be approved by an authority in the country of manufacture.

In some aids part of the buoyancy is provided by air trapped in foam, while further buoyancy can be by air or as gas blown in. In some cases there is no foam and the only buoyancy is due to inflation. Maintenance and servicing checks should be aimed at confirming the efficiency of the safety device.

If air is used, inflate by mouth to the normal pressure and leave some time to see that no air is lost. The usual inflator has a mouthpiece on a tube. This contains a non-return valve and may have a cap. Dip the end of the mouthpiece in water and look for bubbles indicating loss of air. A very slight loss may be acceptable as the wearer can top up during a long immersion. Many aids depend on rubberized fabric to hold the air in. A general loss of air without a definite puncture being obvious may mean deterioration of the fabric, for which there is no cure and the aid should be destroyed rather than discarded and chance that someone else may believe it is still safe. A puncture may be repaired with the materials sold for mending air beds.

Plastic foam buoyant material is not usually accessible in a sound aid, but it can be felt through the fabric casing. It should be quite flexible and there should be no feel of water. It should be securely held in place with very little movement inside the casing.

If a lifejacket uses carbon dioxide gas from a small cartridge to provide rapid inflation in an emergency, it will also have provision for mouth inflation, so the air tightness can be tested without using the CO_2 cartridge. Unfortunately the only way of checking the action of a cartridge is to use it, which means another one has to be fitted. However, if the cartridge is of unknown age or has passed the time allowed by the makers, it would be advisable to have a trial gas inflation, then fit a new cartridge.

Any sort of safety device is of little use if it does not stay in position when the wearer falls into the water. Check all straps, buckles and fasteners. Look for strained stitching. See that fasteners are secure and do not slip at any point of their adjustment. Some may move at the more usually situated fixing position. If a waistcoat type of buoyancy aid depends on lacing, see that the cord is sound and firmly attached at one end. Eyelets or grommets should not have pulled. If they have, replacements may be needed. Be suspicious of any strained stitching.

It is a requirement of the lifejacket specification that there is a strong loop in the front of the harness where the weight of the wearer can be taken to haul him out of the water. If this is ever seriously used, the load can be considerable and the construction and attachment of this loop should be checked, with the probable load in mind, and reinforcing stitching used if there is any doubt.

Repairs may be made to straps and other parts of any harness with sail twine. Be careful if the actual aid needs re-sewing, particularly if it uses inflation. Sewing of a part containing foam should be done very carefully in order to avoid penetrating any inner container.

The most satisfactory test of a lifejacket or buoyancy aid is to try it on a person in the water, and it is good practice to do this at least once a year. So far as possible, simulate unconsciousness with a lifejacket and see that it turns the body face-up. With any type of aid, give rather more than an in-and-out immersion test, as more prolonged use will show if there is water seepage, loosening of straps or other faults not immediately obvious.

A safety device is obviously not something with which chances can be taken, so if an aid is no longer fully satisfactory, it is wisest to replace it. Many jackets suffer from misuse, such as use as cushions on rough surfaces. For some lifejackets there are optional covers. One of these does much to prolong the life of a new lifejacket.

see also BUOYANCY, RESERVE; LIFEBUOYS.

Perspex (Fig. 41)

In boats transparent acrylic resin with this trade name is used for windows, windscreens and similar purposes as an alternative to glass. It is not so easily broken and it can be cut, drilled and shaped with common hand tools. Besides the clear transparent form there are coloured opaque and transparent versions. Commonly available material is in sheet only and most of this is 3 mm (⅛ in) thick. New Perspex is supplied with its highly polished surfaces protected by paper lightly stuck on and this should be left in place as long as possible while working the material.

A new Perspex window should pass more light than glass, but as the material is much softer than glass it soon loses its flawless surface. Dirty Perspex may be washed with warm water and detergent. Window cleaners intended for glass are not very effective on it and any that contain a mild abrasive that would not mark glass should not be used on this softer material.

There are special Perspex polishes. The finer of the two can be used to put a gloss back on a generally dull surface. If there are definite scratches or abraded marks, use the coarser polish, followed by the fine one. If these are unavailable a polish intended for silver can be used for light polishing. One intended for brass is coarser and may remove deeper marks. If this is ineffective on bad markings, use a damp cloth and pumice powder or a household scouring powder. Any coarse cleaning materials must be removed, then a finer cleaner used to remove the marks of the coarser cleaner, and so on if a series of cleaners are used.

None of the usual adhesives will join Perspex parts securely. Use Perspex cement or the product of another manufacturer that specifies this material. The cement softens joining edges so they run together. Use only a small amount on the actual meeting edges. Any excess will mar a surface, even when wiping off immediately.

Heat softens Perspex. Some grades will soften enough to manipulate after soaking in near boiling water. Other grades need the heat of an oven. The material can be pulled to moderate curves, such as a cabin side, and held to shape without internal stresses causing trouble. If Perspex is softened by heat, it can be made sufficiently pliable to take compound curves, but as the surfaces are quite soft, it is difficult to retain their smoothness. For a simple curve, such as a navigation light, a wood former can be covered with soft leather or baize and the soft Perspex laid gently around it with leather gloves (A). When the material cools it will hold its shape.

The effect of heat must be kept in mind when working Perspex. It is generally better to use hand tools than power tools. The friction created by a power tool may generate enough heat for the edge against the tool to melt and either grip the tool so the material breaks or cause cracks to appear. Even if this does not happen the edge left after heating may be very rough.

A fine tenon or hack saw will cut Perspex. A sharp metal-soled plane will true an edge, but most shaping is done with a fine file. This can be followed with abrasive paper (glass and garnet paper are suitable, but avoid emery

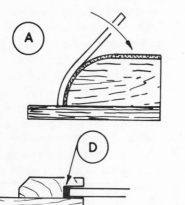
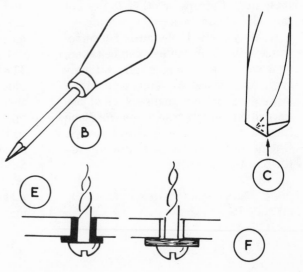

Fig. 41

cloth). If the edge has to be given a polish, follow the finest abrasive paper with successively finer polishing compounds. It is possible to use a power polishing buff, but the correct compound is needed on a mop that has not been used for metal, with light pressure and plenty of movement to avoid local heating.

It is drilling Perspex that sometimes gives trouble. Use a hand wheel brace – never a power drill. Mark the centre with an awl with a square or triangular point (B). Do not use a centre punch. Ordinary metalworking twist drills up to about 4 mm (³⁄₁₆ in) can be turned slowly and with just enough pressure to keep them cutting. Have the Perspex supported so the drill breaks through into wood.

An ordinary metalworking drill in larger sizes tends to dig into the Perspex, which seizes on it and usually cracks. There are special drills with steep flutes for plastic drilling that do not have this failing, but a metalworking drill can be modified by grinding its two cutting edges vertical (C). It is helpful to first go through with a small pilot drill to guide the large drill. Breaking through is the problem time, so have a close wood support behind the Perspex.

It is unwise to have anything too closely fitted to Perspex. If it fits into a groove there may be a rubber sleeve, or there can be a pad of jointing compound (D). If a screw goes through a hole, let the hole be oversize. Use a soft rubber grommet (E) or put a fibre washer under the screw head (F). This is particularly important where the Perspex is pulled to a curve, as in a cabin side window.

Plywood

Plywood is made by bonding together layers of veneer at right-angles to each other. Many qualities and types of wood are used and there are several glues. The majority of plywoods used ashore are unsuitable for use afloat. It is important that the glue should be waterproof and for structural parts of a boat the wood used for all veneers should be suitable for marine use and be of good quality throughout.

British marine-quality plywood complies with British Standard Specification 1088. Imported plywood does not have this marking, but may comply with a standard in the country of manufacture. Exterior plywood has a water-resistant glue, but the quality of the veneers is not up to that of BSS1088 plywood. It may be satisfactory to use exterior plywood for internal parts of a cabin boat that do not have to contribute strength to the boat, but otherwise all plywood used should be a marine grade.

There is always an odd number of plies, so the grain of the outside ones are the same way. The woods normally used have a red tinge, but are not necessarily mahogany. Thicknesses are from 3 mm (⅛ in) upwards. Standard sheets are 8 ft by 4 ft or close metric equivalents. Normal plywood has equal strength all ways, but there are plywoods with greater strength one way, for use where this is an advantage, as in centreboards.

Thicker manufactured boards using solid cores, such as blockboard and laminboard, are not made in marine grades.

see also PLYWOOD REPAIRS.

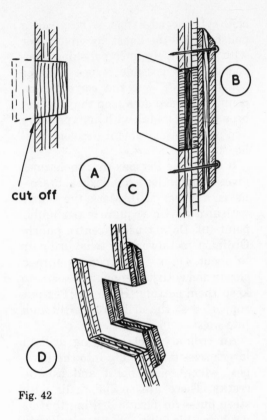

Plywood repairs (Fig. 42)

If a plywood hull or other part of a boat is damaged it is normally repaired with wood, but it is possible to use glassfibre. Small leaks can be sealed with a waterproof stopping or a mixture of glue and sawdust.

A small hole can be trimmed to an even shape, then a solid wood plug with slightly tapered sides driven in with glue (A), and the outside cleaned off flush with the skin. Larger damage on a reasonably flat part may have a piece of plywood fitted in and a backing piece used inside (B). Trim the damage to shape and make a filler to fit it. Make the backing piece to overlap about 25 mm (1 in) all round. Remove any paint or varnish from around the inside of the hole. Glue the backing piece in

Fig. 42

place. If possible, use a strut from somewhere else in the boat to press the backing piece tight while the glue sets. Alternatively, use thin copper or brass nails (C). When the glue has set, cut off the projecting ends. Glue in the repair piece, then sand the outside level and repaint or varnish.

If there is much curve at the point being repaired and the damage is too great to repair with glassfibre, make a backing piece with its centre removed

(D), so it will pull to shape. If possible, make the filler of two thicknesses, so it bends and laminates into shape more easily than a single thickness. Nails may be needed to get and hold the curve.

A cut-out backing piece may also be used for a larger repair, even if there is not much curve. For very extensive damage, it is better to cut away a panel to surrounding supports, such as frames, gunwale and stringers, otherwise the repair may finish flat and the hull shape be spoiled. A repair of this size is best left to an expert.

see also BUOYANCY, RESERVE; GLASS-FIBRE; PLYWOOD.

Polishes

No surface is without flaws, but when the flaws are too fine to be seen in the normal way, it is considered polished. With many materials that are hard enough and have no pores, such as metals and plastics, the surface is broken down with successively finer abrasives until marks from them are too fine to be seen. Some very fine abrasives used in the final stages are rouge and crocus powder. The finer polishes for boat work are in liquid form. A polish for brass is coarser than one for silver, so a brass polish can be followed by a silver polish on any metal for the finest polish. All traces of one abrasive or polish should be wiped or brushed off before moving to a finer one.

Although wood and other porous material can be smoothed with abrasives, any polish has to be applied. On furniture this may be a coating of wax or shellac, which is then rubbed smooth. These finishes do not stand up well afloat. Instead, we use varnish and paint. Epoxy and some other synthetic finishes dry so hard that they can be polished with fine abrasives similar to those used on metals.

When a surface that was polished has deteriorated it can be revived with prepared polishes that may contain a solvent to remove film, a fine abrasive to renew the smoothness and a wax or other coating for protection. Some car polishes of this type may be used on boat metalwork and hard paint finishes.

see also ABRASIVES.

Preservatives

Although it is possible to make water- and rot-proofing solutions, it is simpler and preferable to buy a proprietary brand. Some of the traditional tarlike mixtures for wood and tanning solutions for sails may do their job, but they do not allow for any subsequent treatment. There are chemical solutions, that may be clear or coloured, which are cleaner to use and can be painted over.

Check the intended use on the can or in the maker's brochure. As soakage varies between materials, and soakage is what you want, it is usually wisest to assume that coverage will be much less than is quoted.

Canvas and rope are best soaked in the solution. Although synthetics do not rot, there is an advantage in proofing nylon to reduce its tendency to absorb a small amount of moisture. Some proofing solutions are inflammable and unpleasant if inhaled, so take the precautions recommended by the makers. Proofing solution can be brushed on canvas, but it is difficult to achieve an even appearance on coloured canvas. Spraying will result in a more even colour but may not achieve as good a penetration. Aerosol sprays may be used for touching up or treating small areas, but the amount of proofing solution involved is too small to make this method of application economical for large areas.

Allow treated rope or canvas to dry in an airy place before stowing away.

The problem with treating wood is in getting a sufficient penetration. Preservative on the surface may be better than none, but it is better to get the solution into the grain. Deep penetration of close-grained hardwood may be difficult, but it does not take a thin solution long to pass along the grain of softwoods. Penetration across the grain is slow.

Wood may be stood with its end in proofing solution for some time and there will be a good soakage along the grain. With wood that is already built in, it may be possible to drill holes across the grain and inject preservative repeatedly. If joints are cut or bolt holes drilled, the exposed end grain should be allowed to soak up preservative. If glue is to be used, check that the preservative will not affect its holding power. To be effective, quick application of one coat of preservative is not much use. Repeated application, soaking, injecting plus patience are needed.

Proofing solutions will keep moisture in as well as out, so make sure wood or canvas is really dry before treating. If rot has already taken hold, a preservative may do something to stop its spread, but once decay has taken place, nothing will reverse the process.

see also CANVAS; ROT; VENTILATION.

Propeller

In use, a propeller is liable to hit debris which damages it. This may only be at the edges of the blades and it can be remedied by filing followed by abrasive paper. Do not take off much. It may be better to leave a blade with a nick in the edge than to reduce the diameter so the propeller becomes out of balance. Vibration, particularly at higher speeds, may be due to a propeller out of balance, caused by a knock altering the angle of a blade or breaking away part of it. This cannot be corrected with amateur equipment, but will need expert attention.

Most outboard motor propellers take their drive from the shaft through a shear pin. For an inboard installation there is more likely to be a key, sliding inward in shaft and propeller. If the propeller is removed be careful not to lose the strip of metal which forms the key. There is unlikely to be any need for servicing here, but when reassembling be careful to ensure that all parts are clean and lightly greased.

Folding and variable-pitch propellers are best left alone if they are operating well, except for examining parts for wear and dealing with damaged edges in the same way as for fixed propellers. If there is an operating mechanism through a hollow shaft, this will depend for watertightness and smoothness of operation on packing with grease. Use the grease recommended by the makers, or a waterproof grease as near as possible to the type already in use.

see also OUTBOARD MOTORS; SHEAR PINS.

Purchase (Fig. 43)

There are several arrangements on board that provide assistance so loads greater than could be applied directly can be handled. When lifting heavy weights, such as an engine or mast, during maintenance, it is useful to know how to apply leverage or gain purchase. An appreciation of the means of gaining purchase may help in modifying or improvising a system. A simple example is putting a dinghy on a car roof. If one end is put on first, then the other end lifted to slide it on, little more than half the weight is lifted at one time and the purchase gained is near 2:1

Mechanical advantage is accompanied by limited movement, so no more advantage should normally be arranged than is necessary to make the load to be applied reasonable. Anyone who has handled a multi-part main sheet knows that for a small movement of the boom, a lot of rope has to be pulled through.

A block may merely alter the direction of a rope (A). If the arrangement is reversed and the block attached to the load (B) you have a 2:1 purchase. This still applies if another block is introduced (C). The second block merely alters the direction of the rope. This gives a clue to a guide to leverage. Count the number of parts coming from the moving block and that is the ratio of the purchase gained. Tackle rigged one way may have a ratio of 3:1 (D), while turned end for end it goes up to 4:1 (E).

Levers also provide purchase. Quite a large boat ashore can be moved by one man with a crowbar. The lever bears on

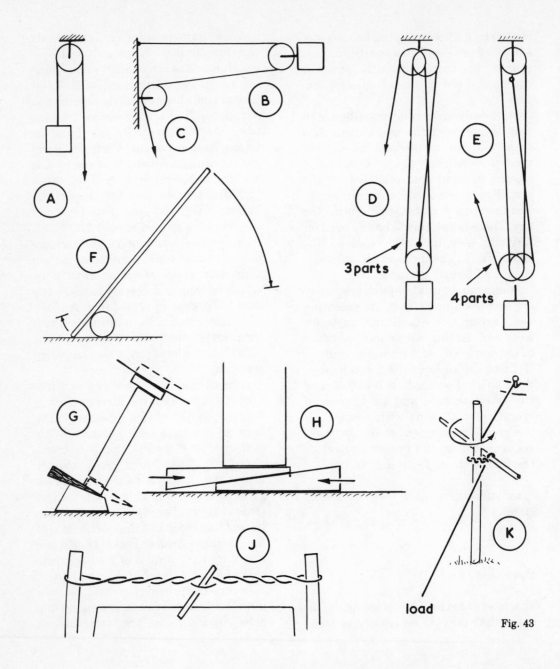

A

B

C

D 3 parts

E 4 parts

F

G

H

J

K

load

Fig. 43

something as a fulcrum, then a comparatively light load moved a long way on the long end applies a very much greater load through a short distance at the other end (F). With a crowbar, the heel of the bent end provides the fulcrum.

Wedges are another way of applying considerable pressure through a short distance. A single wedge may be all that is needed (G). If a parallel drive is needed, use folding wedges (H). The two wedges driven against each other do not move the direction of thrust that a single wedge may.

Twisting rope will provide purchase. A Spanish windlass has several turns and a lever used to twist (J). This is useful for such things as pulling a stubborn piece of wood to shape, as it can be taken up a little at a time as the wood becomes more amenable.

A variation can be used for pulling, such as a boat up a ramp where the surface is too muddy to take a car. A slack rope goes from the boat to the car hitch. A lever is twisted into it and this is worked around a pole held upright (K). The smaller the diameter of the pole, the greater the leverage.

Reefing gear (Fig. 44)

If a main sail has conventional reef points, the parts that suffer greatest strain are the reef cringles (A). Check for security. Additional stitching may be needed. The reef points should be knotted through eyelets or sewn to the sail. Their ends should be examined and whippings renewed if necessary. If synthetic line is used, seal the ends with a flame as well as whipping.

For simple dinghy roller reefing, where the boom is pulled aft and turned by hand before pushing forward again on to a square part of the gooseneck, the first part to wear is usually the square hole in the metal part on the boom. If this has worn out of shape, there may have to be a new fitting or a plate can be screwed or riveted over it (B).

Where the boom is turned by a handle or lever, the mechanism should be checked for functioning and play. Grease can be used on enclosed gears, but this should be sparing if they are open. Where axles can be withdrawn, graphited grease can be introduced during re-assembly. With a lever action there may be a hooked pawl engaging with a sprocket. If they can be adjusted in relation to each other excessive wear

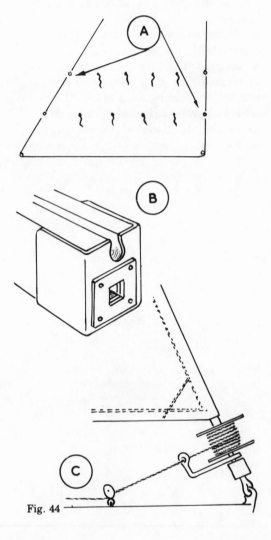

Fig. 44

146

of the sprocket teeth can be reduced. The end of the pawl may need filing to a better hook shape if it is worn. If the handle or lever is removeable, make sure it has a safe stowage nearby.

There are several types of fore sail reefing or furling, but most are operated by a line around a drum at the bottom (C). If the boat is laid up or out of use for some time take the sail off and store it open after washing and drying it, otherwise it may become distorted if left tightly rolled while damp and dirty.

The foresail furling gear relies on several bearings that will require lubricating. The line around the drum may have become worn and need replacing or turning end-for-end to give it a longer life. See that it has a fairlead and does not chafe on the edge of the drum. A block or eye on the deck may be needed to direct the pull.

If the luff of the fore sail is attached to a rod or tube, around which it winds, examine the method of attachment for the whole length. Test the pull of the sheet for direction, and try the action of the furling gear, both for setting by pulling the sheet and reefing or furling by pulling the line on the drum. Easy action of the top bearing attached to the halyard is very important, otherwise the sail may be twisted to an unsatisfactory shape as the bottom rolls more than the top.

see also CANVAS REPAIRS; ROPE; SAIL CARE.

Remote controls

An inboard or outboard engine can be operated by controls directly on it and this is usual for the smallest boats. A change to remote controls allows steering from a more convenient position in larger craft and is essential in some circumstances unless another person is stationed at the engine, with communication from the helmsman. If remote controls are used, it is advisable to retain the direct controls at the engine, so they can be used in emergency and the connections to the remote controls quickly cast off. This means that in routine servicing, the functioning of direct controls should also be checked.

The primary remote control is of the throttle. There have been foot-operated versions, but this is nearly always a hand control. There should also be a gear-change lever, giving forward–neutral–reverse. In some systems a single lever controls both functions. There may also be a car-type switch to control starting and stopping. For some outboard motors the only electrical control is a stop button, which shorts the ignition. There may be a remote choke control, but this is unusual.

Older installations used rods and linkage, with a system of cranks, possibly with chain and cable. This soon developed play and backlash. Inefficiency in these controls could lead to a dangerous situation and it would be better to replace such a system with modern push–pull cables.

In a push–pull cable system it is important that the cable should follow easy curves and not be forced to conform to shape any more than necessary. During inspection, observe the behaviour of the cable casing when the control is operated. If it tries to bow or flex against attachment points, they may not be in the best places and should be changed. If it is an outboard motor see that there is enough looped cable forward of the motor to allow proper control at any position of the motor. Large natural curves reduce friction in the cable and make for easy smooth control.

Check the movement of the throttle hand lever and the movement at the engine throttle, with and without the remote control attached. If the free movement is more than the remote control allows, there is something wrong with the adjustment, usually by screw on the cable end or at the hand control.

With the gear-change control, the important thing is a clean move into a definite neutral. If the engine cannot be put into neutral with certainty, the boat might sometimes be in a tricky and dangerous situation. Observe what happens at the engine and at the hand control and make any adjustments each way from neutral. If it is a combined throttle and gear control in one lever, it is advisable to read the installation sheet or handbook before making adjustments. Be careful not to disturb the override lever action (if there is

one), that permits some throttle opening while the engine is in neutral, for a cold start.

Many push–pull controls are lubricated during manufacture and may need no further treatment, but check with the maker's instructions. In some systems there are grease points along the casing. Push–pull action without slackness or backlash depends on secure anchoring of the casing as well as the cable. See that the ends of the casing and any mounting brackets cannot move. This can be checked by watching the cable casing end as the lever is moved backwards and forwards. If the case around the lever(s) is opened, the moving parts will be found to be lubricated with grease. There should be enough, but avoid over-lubricating or using a very liquid lubricant, which may leak out and soil clothes. Water-resistant grease as used from a tube for the gear box of some outboard motors is suitable.

If there are remote electrical controls, check insulation of the cable and switch, see that all wires of a flexible cable are making a good contact and any clips holding the electric cable to the hull are secure and not chafing the cable insulation. Clean switch contacts, if they have become damaged by arcing.

see also FUEL SYSTEM; INBOARD ENGINES, PETROL.

Rigging, running (Fig. 45)

The ropes that control sails may be fibre or wire rope or a combination of the two. Wire rope presents less windage and it is free from stretch, so sails can be set up taut. Its flexibility is limited and it cannot be handled satisfactorily, so wire rope is found in halyards for the part that takes the strain, while there may be a fibre rope tail for handling when hoisting. For sheets and other ropes that have to be handled it is unusual for there to be any wire rope in their length. There are synthetic fibre ropes with negligible stretch, so the advantages of including wire rope in halyards is not so great as when soft ropes were made of natural fibres.

There are now plaited or braided ropes that are more comfortable to handle than stranded rope, and normally smooth continuous filaments can be treated to give the hairy feel of natural fibre rope for a better grip. These ropes should be chosen for replacement sheets. Although quite a thin rope may have sufficient strength, a comfortable and secure grip can only be obtained on rope 9 mm (⅜ in) or preferably 12 mm (½ in) thick.

Natural fibre rope suffers from rot. This can be seen by twisting a three-strand rope open. Pronounced blackness inside means rot. Synthetic rope does not suffer from rot, but examine it for wear. If it has been used in a salty atmosphere, wash it with fresh water. Dirty rope can be washed in a bucket of warm water and weak detergent, but afterwards swill or hose with fresh water and hang the rope to dry. Salt in rope attracts moisture from the atmosphere and the rope may never completely dry.

The greater part of many ropes used for hoisting or controlling sails have

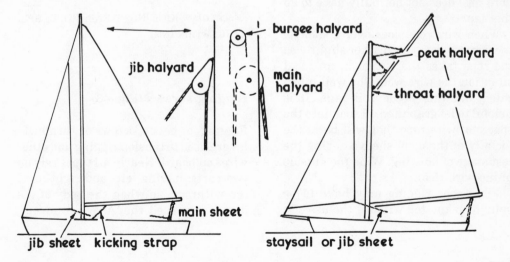

Fig. 45

done their work when the sail is set and only a short part is under load. It is good practice to turn such a rope end for end periodically to even the strain and wear. If a rope for a particular purpose has to be scrapped because of wear or chafe, it may be possible to use a sound part for another purpose, which is a reason for keeping the various items of running rigging the same section if possible.

Flexible wire rope used for halyards may have a long life, but the part which may wear first is the short length next to the sail where the rope is curved over the mast sheave. The larger this sheave is, the longer the wire rope will last, but there are practical limitations and the sheave may not be as big as might be desirable. Whatever its size, a groove section to match the wire rope size is desirable, but if there is a fibre rope tail to follow the wire over the sheave, the groove must be larger. In some rigs the fibre rope does not normally have to go that far.

When wire rope goes over a sheave, the wires slide on each other slightly as the rope takes the curve. In an ideal situation the wire would be well lubricated, but this would soil sails. It is helpful to let graphited oil soak into the spaces of wire rope that will be in the vicinity of the mast sheave during the last stage of hoisting. Wipe the outside of the wire clean.

Fibre rope rigging may have to be spliced or knotted without the use of a thimble in some circumstances, but where a thimble can be used, it is better for the rope. The free end of a rope should be both sealed and whipped. Some synthetic rope will unlay rapidly if an end is left to its own devices. This could extend some distance and it is usually impossible to lay up again as neatly as the manufactured lay, so check whippings and replace them if necessary and further seal any doubtful ends.

Local wear on running rigging may be due to badly designed or incorrectly positioned fittings. If it is a class boat, alterations should not be made until rules have been checked to see that classification would not be affected. Otherwise, it may be possible to reposition fairleads or cleats, round edges or change fittings completely to give a better run or action of the sheets or halyards, so wear does not occur on a replacement rope.

see also KICKING STRAP; ROPE; SPLICING; WHIPPING.

Rigging screws (Fig. 46)

Rigging, or bottle, screws or turnbuckles are used to tension rigging and other wires on board. Nearly all types rely on two parts, having left- and right-hand screw thread, so when the body of the device is turned they move in or out.

Ends are various to suit applications. It is important that the pull is direct, particularly when there is no flexibility due to a shackle between parts. A chainplate or similar fitting should be bent to match a fork end on a rigging screw (A).

Some rigging screws have no means of locking. They can be wired, with the wire arranged in the direction that resists unscrewing (B). Some rigging screws are provided with locknuts at one or both ends. A nut to take a spanner (C) is better than the knurled nut sometimes provided. It is usually possible to put a nut on the right-hand threaded end, even if one was not provided originally. Where the body of the fitting is open, the ends of the screws may be drilled to take wires (D). Even when locknuts are provided, it may be advisable to use wire as well. Any roughness that might damage sails can be covered by binding with self-adhesive tape.

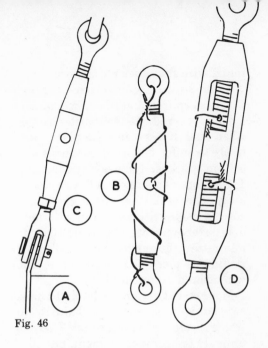

Fig. 46

Rigging, standing (Fig. 47)

It is unusual for any boat today to have fibre rope standing rigging, and with modern wire rope available it may be advisable to replace any fibre rope with wire, even on the smallest dinghy. Although some fibre ropes are without noticeable stretch, wire is more rigid and offers less windage.

The best way to gain the maximum strength from a given cross-section of wire is to have it in a single piece. Such 'rod-rigging' has been used, but problems come in fixing and dismantling, due to the lack of flexibility, so it may kink and cannot usually be rolled. Most wire rigging in the past has been seven-strand, with six strands around a central straight strand, which was sometimes hemp. This was protected by galvanizing and was often iron. Later rigging was similar, but of steel, and like that used for running rigging. More recently, stainless steel has been used and is now often nineteen-strand for both standing and running rigging. Seven and nineteen are the chosen figures because of the geometry of the cross-sections – they make up into a round wire that does not distort.

Seven-strand galvanized rigging wire was spliced and the splice parcelled and served. Deterioration comes when rust attacks and the place most likely to suffer first is in the tucks of a bottom splice, so remove any covering. The action of splicing will have chipped away some of the zinc coating so slight rusting is inevitable, although there may be tar or a mastic compound used to minimize attack under the parcelling. If rusting is more than superficial, the wire should be replaced.

More recent rigging is likely to have swaged splices, such as Talurit, in which a collar is squeezed on. There is unlikely to be any movement, but slipping would be obvious. Except for inspection, there is no maintenance for stainless steel wire spliced in this way. If there is a screwed connection on the end of the wire (e.g. Norseman, or similar), it is not recommended that the fitting should be opened for examination. If a fitting is opened, possibly for re-use on a shortened wire, check the maker's instructions, as an internal part may have to be replaced. Fittings are for one size and type of wire, usually nineteen-strand, and cannot be transferred to another type.

Avoid kinking rigging wire. If it is taken off for storage, coil in large loops. Kinked wire has been weakened and should not be trusted. Examine stranded wire rope for broken wires in a strand, which can be felt by rubbing a hand along. One or two broken single wires at long intervals may not matter, but they are a sign that the rope may have to be replaced before very long.

Rigging that does not have fitted ends should normally have eyes around metal thimbles. Plastic thimbles are unsuitable for wire. Wire rope without a

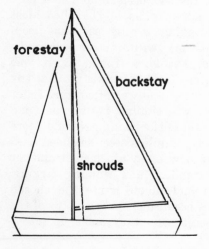

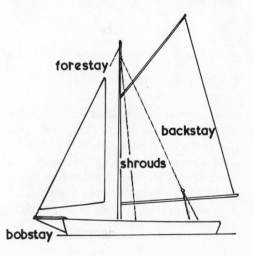

Fig. 47

152

thimble may pull so the eye is elongated and the curve that takes the load is too small a radius, so separate wires break. This may also happen if the thimble is made of thin sheet metal. Wire rope under strain should be maintained at a moderate curve and not allowed to distort. The groove around a thimble should match the size of wire and to prevent it elongating, it would be best made of solid metal with only a hole drilled to take the shackle pin or other attachment.

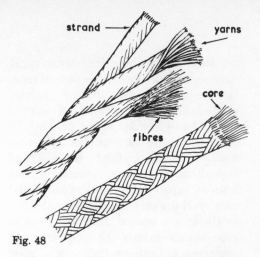

Fig. 48

Rope (Fig. 48)

Traditionally, ropes for use afloat have been made of such natural fibres as hemp and manila for the better ropes, coir where the rope was required to float and sisal for cheaper ropes. Cotton was used for soft flexible ropes such as sheets. Although these materials may be met, nearly all modern yachting ropes are made of synthetic materials, and are recommended for replacements. The general-purpose good-quality yachting rope is polyester (e.g. Terylene; Dacron). This has negligible stretch, does not absorb water and does not rot. There are polypropylene and other synthetics with similar qualities, but these ropes are usually of lesser strength. Nylon rope is slightly absorbent, but does not rot. It is elastic and therefore unsuitable for halyards, but it

is suitable for mooring lines and anchor cables.

Synthetic fibres can be produced in many ways so they may be difficult to identify in ropes. Normal construction uses continuous filaments so there is none of the hairiness (due to the short fibres) found in ropes made from natural materials. However, ropes of synthetic material may be made with shorter pieces to give the hairy grip. These ropes may be described as 'spun' or 'stapled'.

Most ropes, whether natural or synthetic fibre, are three-strand and laid up right-handed – as you look along the rope it twists away from you clockwise, to the right. The yarns in each strand twist the other way and the fibres making up the yarns twist right-handed. It is this alternate twisting that helps the rope keep its shape. Plaited or braided rope has a smoother exterior and a more comfortable grip. The outside is made up of yarns plaited

153

together. Inside there may be straight yarns or a form like a three-strand rope. Double-braided rope has a second plaited layer. There are left-handed ropes, four-stranded ropes and others made up to give various effects, but for most ropework afloat three-strand right-handed rope is usual, with braided ropes where ease of handling, easy working through blocks and other qualities are needed. Size and type of rope should match the original in a replacement, unless there is a good reason for doing otherwise.

Rope sizes are now given in millimetres diameter. Until metrication, sizes were for circumference in inches and fractions. There is a convenient conversion: the number of ⅛ in in the circumference is the same as the number of millimetres in the diameter. For example: 1½ in (12 eighths) circumference equals 12 mm diameter. The table shows approximate breaking strains for comparison.

Heat will melt synthetic fibre ropes, so friction as well as direct heat should be avoided. Natural fibres burn instead of melting. Ends of synthetic ropes should be sealed with heat. This can be done with a flame, such as a match or cigarette lighter. After the end has softened, roll it between a moistened finger and thumb. This should be done to the ends of strands before splicing. As many stranded synthetic fibre ropes will unlay rapidly if left free, and are very difficult to put together again, sealing immediately after cutting is important. It is usual to back up a sealed end with a whipping for a permanent end treatment. Rope may be cut with a special tool which includes a heated knife, so the parted ends are sealed as they are cut.

see also KNOTS; REEFING GEAR; RIGGING, RUNNING; SPLICING.

TABLE OF APPROXIMATE BREAKING STRAINS OF ROPE, TO SHOW COMPARATIVE STRENGTHS.

	Diameter (mm)							
	6	8	9	10	12	14	16	18
Manila	800	1200	1500	1950	2650	3450	4400	5400
Nylon	1800	2900	4000	5400	7100	8900	11000	15000
Polyester	1800	2900	3800	5200	6500	8300	10400	14400
Polypropylene	1250	1850	2600	3400	4150	4900	5900	7900
Sisal	730	1000	1300	1700	2100	2800	3900	4500

Rot

There are several forms of rot, but to the boat owner they all produce the same problem. Rot is a fungus which attacks natural materials. Synthetic materials are not attacked, although the fungus may sometimes be found on the surface. Fungal decay or rot in a wooden boat can be serious, involving the removal of a considerable amount of material or the writing-off of the whole boat. The cause of most rot is moisture with lack of ventilation. Trapped water or stagnant moist air encourages rot. Adequate ventilation is the best preventative. Salt water is a mild fungicide, so rot is less likely if it is salt water that is trapped. Rot needs oxygen from the air, so rot is unlikely in waterlogged conditions, such as the bottom of the bilges. Rainwater leaking through decks and then becoming trapped may cause rot.

Besides wood, rot can be a problem with sails and ropes made from natural materials. Mildew is a mild form of rot, which may not seriously affect the strength of natural fibre sails, but it is disfiguring. Its appearance can be improved by treating with dilute domestic bleach, but this may affect any dye in the sail. Natural fibre materials should be treated with a preservative that discourages rot.

Besides compartments and lockers where water may be trapped there are gaps under paint films, spaces behind rubbing strips or under fittings where water may lie and rot commence. A jointing compound should be used to bed these things in place if they are not closely glued. There is no problem with any part becoming wet, so long as it can dry out in a reasonable time, so rot is unusual in above-deck woodwork which is exposed to wind.

Woods have different resistances to rot. In general, softwoods are more susceptible to attack than hardwoods. Teak is one of the most durable. Mahogany is a good choice, while beech and ash, which have uses ashore, may not last long afloat. Although preservatives can be applied to woodwork during maintenance, it is really only possible to achieve a good penetration on new wood before it is built in.

Once rot has taken hold, the spores of the fungus spread quickly. There are special synthetic resins that can be injected into rotten wood. These harden in the wood and kill the spores, but they have limited use. The usual treatment has to be more drastic. Wood that has been attacked must be removed and burned immediately, otherwise spores may float in the air and contaminate other wood. To be certain, it is necessary to go about 50 cm (20 in) along the grain past the last sign of decay and 10 cm (4 in) away across the grain. All of this has to be cut out and destroyed. Whether it is practicable and the boat will be worth rebuilding depends on particular circumstances, but there is no simple way of eradicating rot.

The surrounding remaining area should be treated with preservative and this should be used on all new wood being built in.

Rot in natural fibre rope or canvas needs similar treatment to wood. Rope that is affected is probably best destroyed and replaced. Do not be tempted to keep the decaying rope for a lesser use, as the spores may pass to sound fibres of rope, canvas or wood. It will also be wisest to scrap and destroy a rotten sail, even if part seems sound. If an apparently sound part is salvaged for further use, treat it thoroughly with preservative, preferably by soaking.

see also CANVAS; PRESERVATIVES; VENTILATION.

Rowlocks (crutches) (Fig. 49)

A metal rowlock can soon damage an oar, even when the latter is leathered, so it is important to check inside a rowlock for roughness, which can be corrected by filing and the use of abrasive. Some rowlocks pull out of shape in use.

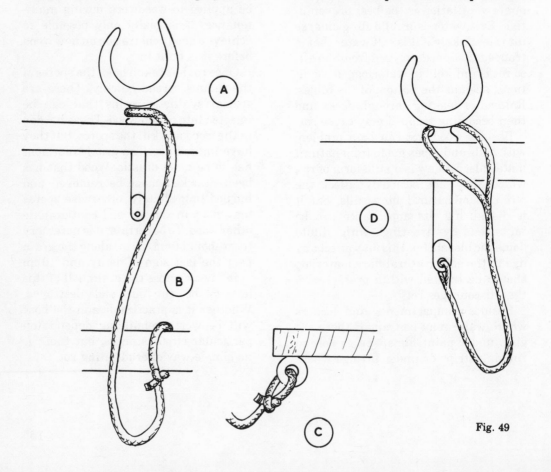

Fig. 49

If there is a high side, hammer its top to a good curve or pull it to shape in a vice. If the top of the rowlock is no more than just wide enough to admit the oar, it will be easier to use. Do not try to bend nylon or other plastic rowlocks.

If the rowlock is not a type that locks in its socket or swings down out of use, it should be fitted with a lanyard. This is better around the neck (A) than through the hole at the bottom of the stem. Take the lanyard to the riser under the thwart, if there is one (B), or to an eye under the thwart (C). In any case allow enough length for the rowlock to be lifted out without unfastening the lanyard.

If there is nothing that the end of the lanyard can be fixed to, it may be attached to the bottom of the stem, then a loop spliced with just enough length to go over the top of the rowlock (D).

Rudder (Fig. 50)

The proper functioning of the rudder is vital to any boat. A fault there could lead to the boat going out of control and a dangerous situation developing. Particular care of the rudder and steering arrangements should always be taken.

All of the underwater part of a wooden rudder should be faired off. There is little to be gained by an overall aerofoil section, but the edges should be thinned and it is theoretically best to have the leading edge to a blunt curve and the trailing edge with more taper (A). After a season, the lower part of a wooden blade may be chafed and damaged, so it should be reshaped and thoroughly painted or varnished. Sealing with glassfibre tape and resin may give some protection, but this may rub through after only a little use.

The above-water part of a wooden rudder is unlikely to have suffered, but the action of levering with a tiller puts a considerable strain on cheeks (B) and their condition and security should be checked. Boat nails taken right through and clenched on roves may be better than wood screws if strengthening is required, but nuts and bolts can be used (C).

If the rudder has a lifting wooden blade, check wear at the bolt holes. If it is a bad case, it may be best to enlarge the hole to allow a plug to be glued in and re-drilled for the bolt (D). A piece of metal tube fixed in the hole with epoxy glue will prevent further wear (E). If the lifting blade uses shock cord, it will probably be advisable to replace this during an annual refit. When repainting or varnishing a lifting rudder, dismantle it and make sure the hidden parts get adequate treatment. Water being absorbed into any of the meeting surfaces could cause the wood to swell and interfere with the lifting and lowering of the blade.

Rudder hangings are often neglected. If the rudder hits the bottom or the helm

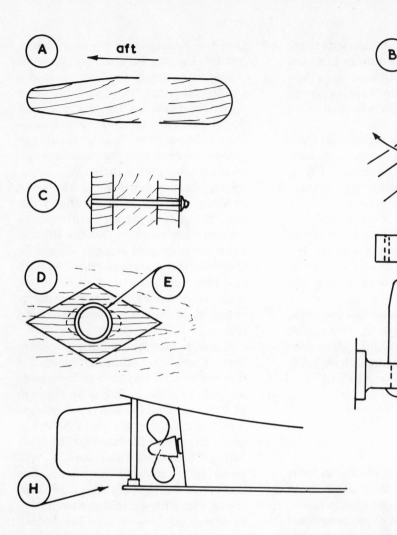

Fig. 50

is put hard over, there is a heavy load put on them and their fastenings, particularly the lower ones. Check screws and bolts. Through fastenings are better than wood screws, even in a small dinghy. Those through the transom should have large washers or drilled metal plates inside to spread the load over a reasonable area of wood. There should be wood or other reinforcement inside a glassfibre transom. If through fastenings are withdrawn and replaced, coat them and the holes with jointing compound.

Play on rudder hangings may not have much effect on steering, except there may be some slack felt when altering the helm, but it is better to have more closely engineered bearings than there sometimes are, even with new gudgeons and pintles. If there is wear in a hole, it may be possible to open it and fit a bush (F). If the pintle has worn, it can be cut off and a new one riveted through (G). However, replacement parts may be preferable.

If a new tiller has to be made from wood, ash is best able to withstand bending strains, but it is not a durable wood in damp conditions so it should be treated with a proofing solution before being painted or varnished. Many other available hardwoods can be used and there is some advantage in strength if several laminations are glued together, then the tiller made from them. These may all be of the same wood, or contrasting colours are attractive. If the tiller is shaped, the laminations should be pulled to shape around a block of wood used as a mould, then cramped to it until the glue has set. This ensures grain following the curve and not being weakened by being cut across if straight wood is used.

The rudder used with an inboard engine installation may be bronze or galvanized steel with a shaft passing up through the hull. The blade should be checked for damage and made good by filing. Most load on the system may be at a bearing below the rudder blade, where the bottom of the rudder shaft turns in the end of a protective strip of metal coming aft from a skeg below the propeller (H). Check the condition of this bearing. If badly worn there may be a risk of separating, so the rudder becomes inoperative, may buckle and could foul the propeller. It may be possible to bush or repair parts, but in a bad case a complete replacement may be avoided by having the worn metal built up professionally.

The shaft passing through the hull usually has bearings top and bottom of a tube. Dismantle and pack with grease if no grease points are provided for lubricating without dismantling. Check the security and proper functioning of the attachment for remote steering and the availability and fitting of an emergency tiller. See that all parts are properly locked and that there is no fear of anything coming apart in use.

see also CENTRE AND DAGGER BOARDS; LAMINATING; WHEEL STEERING.

Sail care

Terylene and nylon sails may be washed with warm water and detergent. This should remove dirt as well as salt. Although it might be possible to put a small sail in a washing machine, it is better to spread it and use the detergent with a cloth or brush. How hard it is rubbed depends on the weight of the sail cloth. Only heavy grades should be scrubbed hard. Others are better wiped. Synthetic cloth does not absorb dirt in the same way that natural fibres do, so cleaning is more on the surface. Follow washing by rinsing with fresh water, which can be hosed on. Hang the sail to dry. Corners and other places with several thicknesses may take several days to dry.

Stains may be tackled before washing. Mildew may be partly removed by brushing. A mild bleach can then be used on it. Rust and some other stains may respond to a 5% solution of oxalic acid and water. Wash with clean water afterwards.

Oil, grease, tar and their derivatives may be removed with white spirit. Place the affected part over a pad of absorbent cloth, so dissolved impurities pass through. A hand-cleaning jelly may also be used. In both cases follow with warm water and detergent to remove the treatment, then use fresh water to remove the detergent.

If sails are stored for some time, it is better to leave them loosely folded than tight in a bag. It is helpful to refold them in different creases occasionally.

see also CANVAS; CANVAS REPAIRS; REEFING GEAR.

Sanding (Fig. 51)

Surfaces, whether bare wood, metal or painted, may be rubbed down with abrasive. Freehand sanding of a shaped surface is acceptable, but for a flat surface it is better to support the abrasive paper or cloth. Most British abrasive sheet is supplied about 28 cm (11 in) by 23 cm (9 in). This is conveniently torn into four, by pulling against a straight-edge (A). The traditional sanding block is cork and of a size that allows the paper to be curved up the side and held; 13 cm (5 in) by 7.5 cm (3 in) is about right. There are metal sanding pads that grip the paper, but cork or wood with a rubber face has the advantage of floating if dropped overboard.

'Wet-and-dry' paper cuts better and

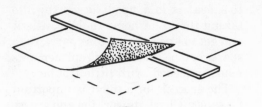

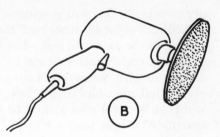

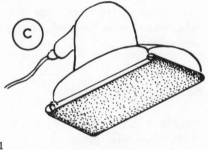

Fig. 51

longer if used damp. Glasspaper normally has a non-waterproof glue so it must be kept very dry if it is to have a reasonable life. Sand in the direction of the grain or the long way of the work if there is no grain. For the finest finish, work through several progressively finer grades of abrasive, but dust or blow away all particles of one abrasive before changing to another.

For power sanding there are rotating sanding pads, orbital sanders and belt sanders. A rotating sanding disc (B) will remove material quickly, but the surface left will show curved marks, which may be difficult to remove. An orbital sander is a flat pad which moves rapidly with a small movement (C). It serves as a substitute for hand-sanding, but is not necessarily any faster. A belt sander uses a continuous belt of abrasive (D). With coarse grit it will rapidly remove material, but with finer grit used in line with the grain it will produce a good finish.

Besides abrasive on sheets, there are alternatives, particularly suitable for the many curves of a boat. Pumice powder or domestic scouring powder can be used on wood, glassfibre or metal. Used

161

dry on a cloth, this will prepare a varnished surface for a further coat. Emery powder can be used with thin oil on steel or other metals. Steel wool can be used dry or with oil or water, but if any particles are left embedded in a surface, they will rust, so steel wool should be used sparingly for boat work.

see also ABRASIVES.

Sanitation

If a portable chemical toilet is used on board there is no maintenance other than flushing out and recharging with the special fluid. If a system with a holding tank is used, emptying and flushing through should not be delayed a long time. Whenever there is an opportunity for pumping out, it should be taken even if the tank will hold more.

If there is a toilet discharging into the water, read the maker's instructions about servicing (data sheets giving part numbers are available), particularly if the pumps and valves are giving trouble. Routine maintenance of a toilet that is working properly consists of cleaning and oiling moving parts. Problems come with leaks past pistons or flap valves that do not close or only partly close. There is little that can be done to the old parts and replacements are advisable, although it is possible to make some parts from sheet neoprene.

If a boat is laid up, it is worthwhile taking the toilet home to dismantle it and get to know the various parts, then spares can be carried and replacements made if needed, with little trouble.

The seacock for a toilet is important for safety. Check its working and grease it. See that all flanges and fastenings are firm.

Because the operation of a sea toilet is different from a household one, maintenance problems will be reduced if operating instructions are displayed where they can be read in the toilet compartment.

Scarfing (Fig. 52)

Glue has a more secure grip on side grain than end grain. A satisfactory glued joint cannot be made with wood end to end. If it is necessary to join two pieces to make up length or to add a new part endwise to an old part during repair, the joint has to be arranged so there is a good area of side grain in contact. With modern glues this can be done with a single scarf, and the recommended angle of scarf is a minimum of 1:7 (A). This applies to solid wood or plywood.

If strips have to be joined to make up length, it is possible to plane both ends at the same time if one is fixed over the other, with the lengths of scarf marked (B) and the two pieces planed together (C). Some of the surplus wood can be

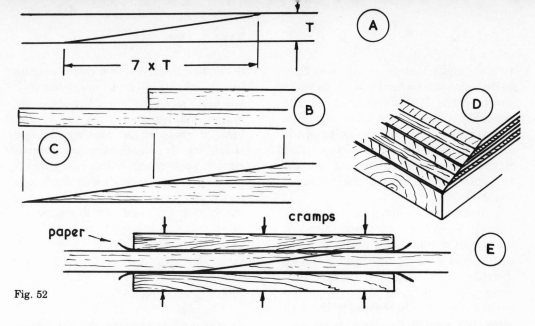

Fig. 52

removed by sawing first. The surface of the bench top should be true and there should be no fear of the lower part flexing as it is planed, otherwise a close-fitting joint will not be made.

It is difficult to keep a scarf joint true over much width of plywood. It is usually unwise to scarf plywood panels over a width much more than 30 cm (12 in) by hand methods. Have a stiff, flat board under the plywood during planing, with its edge supporting what will be a feather edge on the lower piece (D). If wider panels have to be joined it is wiser and gives a more robust finish to let edges butt and have a cover piece inside, than to make an imperfect scarf joint.

When a scarf joint is glued, have stiff boards, long enough to extend some way each side of the joint. Use paper to pre-

vent these pieces sticking to the work. Cramp over the extended parts as well as over the joint (E).

A scarfed joint is stiffer than the adjoining wood. If the wood will be curved, arrange the scarf to come in the part of least curvature. If a curved part is made by laminating and this has to be joined to a straight part, let there be a section of straight on the laminated part, so the scarf does not have to take a curve.

see also ADHESIVES; MASTS; SPARS.

Shackles (Fig. 53)

A collection of spare shackles should be

163

in any boat's bag or repair kit. Normally, a shackle should be as large as can be fitted. If chain is involved, the shackle pin should be at least as thick as a chain link. With other equipment it should be as thick as the thinnest part under load in the item – in a bottle screw it would be as thick as the threaded part.

The hole in the eye of a common shackle is not there for using the point of a marline spike. It is better to use a slotted tool (A) or a pair of pliers. Where security after fitting is more important than the ability to dismantle, the threaded end can be riveted with a ball pane hammer (B). A large shackle may be drilled for a split pin (C). One of these treatments may be used on an anchor. Elsewhere, the pin may be wired through the hole in the eye (D). Keep the wire clear of anything contained in the shackle and bend the twisted ends where they cannot catch on anything.

Shackles are made in many patterns (E) and in the usual metals for marine use. Some rigging items are made with what is really a built-in shackle. During annual maintenance it may be advisable to replace an existing simple shackle with something more appropriate or convenient. A distorted shackle is a danger sign as it is a weak link, and it should be replaced with a larger shackle or one made from a stronger alloy.

Shear pins (Fig. 54)

To prevent the shock of hitting an underwater obstruction being transferred to the drive, the propeller of an outboard motor has to be designed to slip or disengage. Although there are other devices, many makes of outboard motor use a shear pin to transmit the drive from shaft to propeller. This breaks and has to be replaced.

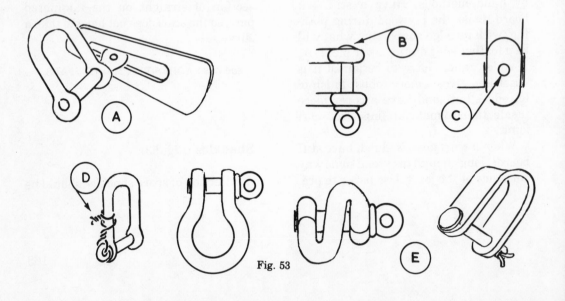

Fig. 53

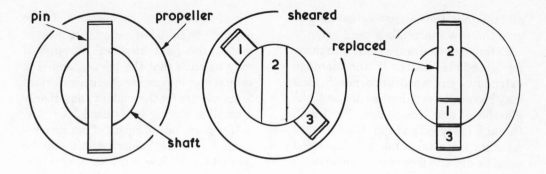

Fig. 54

It is advisable to find out how to replace a shear pin before an emergency arises and a pin should be replaced during routine maintenance if it is found to be bent or partly sheared. Usually the propeller is held on its shaft with a nut, which may be castellated and secured with a split pin. Have spare split pins as one that is straightened and re-bent may break. Sliding the propeller off shows the shear pin through the shaft and grooves in the propeller to engage with it. A new pin will drive out a broken piece. Ideally, correct shear pins should be bought from the motor manufacturer. Alternatively, pieces cut from a nail or mild steel rod of the correct diameter, can be used. If caught without a spare, it is possible to re-arrange the broken pieces to get a drive on one side (see drawing), which will stand up to careful use for a short distance.

see also PROPELLER; SPLIT PINS.

Sheathing

If a wooden hull has been sheathed it is important that the sheathing remains intact, otherwise water getting behind the sheathing may be almost impossible to remove and may cause rot. Worn sheathing should be repaired before there is a hole through it.

Glassfibre cloth with a polyester resin is commonly used, but an epoxy resin may be applied. In the Cascover system, nylon cloth is bedded in resorcinol glue. Any of these systems may be finished with several coats of paint. Anyone familiar with the methods may be able to identify them by examination, but it is advisable to discover the history of the sheathing if possible before repairing. Similar glue and resin should be used if possible. If there is any doubt, it should be safe to use epoxy resin and glass cloth on any of these sheathings. Remove paint before making a repair and roughen the damage by sanding to give the new materials a good grip.

Extensive repairs are similar to those for glassfibre boats. If the damage extends to the wood underneath, this may have to be repaired with wood, but glassfibre and resin can be taken through the wood and the sheathing, so no other material is needed. The wood must be dry and free of paint or varnish if the resin is to bond properly.

Soldering, soft (Fig. 55)

Soft solder is an alloy of lead and tin, which can be used to bond metal to metal. Its mechanical strength is not high, but it will join most metals and alloys, except aluminium and its alloys. Its main use on a boat is in making electrical connections, when the joint will be a better conductor and more permanent than any mechanical clip, screw or spring connector. Copper and alloys containing copper are particularly easy to solder.

Soft solder has to be melted by heat, which can be provided by a flame or a copper bit, often called a 'soldering iron', although the vital part is copper. For small electrical connections amongst other things that would be damaged by a flame, a bit is the usual tool. Where mains electricity is available, an electric soldering bit is convenient and quite a small one is adequate for things of little bulk, like the major-

ity of boat wiring connections. If the object to be soldered has a large mass of metal, the heat dispersal through it may be such that the part intended to take solder may never reach a sufficient temperature for the solder to flow if only a small soldering bit is used.

If you are out of reach of mains electricity, a plain soldering bit can be heated by a blow lamp or over a gas cooker flame and used in the same way. Obviously, it has to be reheated periodically if much soldering is being done.

The meeting surfaces must be reasonably mechanically clean. Rubbing with abrasive cloth or scraping with a knife just before soldering is all that is needed. There has to be a flux to provide chemical cleanliness and help the solder to flow. The flux covers the surfaces and prevents air getting at them and oxidizing them when they become hot. For small electrical connections suitable solder is available as a thick wire with a core containing flux, which flows as the solder melts. This is particularly suitable for electrical parts which may be difficult to clean afterwards, as an excess is avoided and the flux is a non-corrodable type which will do no harm if left.

For larger soldering jobs it is better to buy a liquid or paste flux, which is put on the surfaces with a small brush or stick, and ought to be washed off afterwards.

When a plain soldering bit is heated with a flame, it needs cleaning. This is done by briefly dipping in flux after removing from the flame. The heat required to melt solder is nowhere near red heat. If a bit is very much over-heated, the end will have to be prepared again by filing it bright, heating and dipping in flux before touching with solder to give it a coat all over the work-ing end. So long as the bit is kept within a suitable temperature range, attention to the bit, other than dipping in flux each time, will not be needed. An elec-tric soldering bit is unlikely to over-heat, so the point should remain in good condition almost indefinitely.

To make a small electrical soldered joint, have the cleaned parts touching, then rest the bit on them, so they become hot from it. After a few seconds touch the end of a piece of cored solder on the work and the bit (A). If the heat is sufficient, the solder will melt and flow into the joint. Be careful of overdoing it – withdraw the stick of solder quickly. If the parts are being held by hand, do not let them move and keep holding until the appearance of the solder changes from a shine to a dull surface. This hap-pens quite suddenly.

For a larger joint, put flux along the meeting parts and solder in the same way, but draw the bit along the joint slowly so heat flows into the metal and follow up by feeding plain solder a little at a time (B). Providing the parts are heated enough, solder will flow between quite close meeting surfaces. If the area for soldering is more extensive – say a disc about 25 mm (1 in) across flat on to something – it is advantageous to 'tin' the surfaces first. Before they are brought together, one or both surfaces are coated with flux, then solder spread over them thinly with a hot bit. When the parts are brought together with more flux and again heated, the tinned surfaces will flow together and make the joint.

A flame for soldering needs to be adjustable down to a quite low flame for fine work, although a higher flame is needed when the parts are large and liable to disperse heat quickly. An ordi-nary round flame from a paraffin or gas blowlamp is suitable. The main advan-tage of a flame over a bit is the ability to provide more heat, so larger joints are more easily made. A disadvantage is

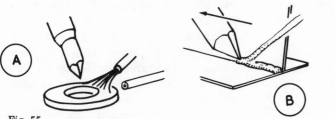
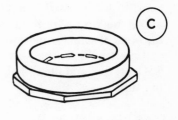

Fig. 55

that the heat cannot be as localized and something that should not get hot may be damaged by heat from flame soldering nearby. When soldering parts with a flame it is helpful to support them on firebrick or something else unaffected by heat, but not by metal, which would draw heat away.

When soldering with a flame it is usual to keep the heat away from the solder. Solder tends to run towards the hottest part when it melts. If the cleaned and fluxed parts are held in contact and heated on one side while solder is fed to the other side, the solder will flow through towards the flame. For most joints, keep the flame moving to produce a general heating rather than just one hot spot. An example is flat plate to seal the end of a tube (C). Clean the meeting surfaces and have the plate slightly oversize. Apply flux and put little pieces of solder around the inside. Hold the parts steady and move the flame around the outside. The solder will melt and run through. Alternatively, do not put pieces of solder inside, but judge when the heat is sufficient and touch the end of the stick of solder to the joint. Solder will then run all round the joint. It is very easy to apply too much solder this way, so be ready to withdraw the stick of solder almost as soon as the end melts. When the joint has cooled, wash off flux and file the plate to match the tube.

see also BRAZING.

Solvents

A number of solvents are used in the upkeep and maintenance of a boat for cleaning and as thinners for paint or other things.

The common thinner for paint is white spirit. Do not use paraffin. A very small amount of thinner can have a considerable effect. As warmth will also make paint more viscous, it may be better to warm paint in cold conditions than to add thinners. Most two-pot paints have their own special thinners. To thin anti-fouling will reduce its effectiveness, so should not be done.

Methylated spirit (alcohol) can be used to dissolve many things, including inks, wax polish, some food stains and shellac.

Paraffin will remove oil or dilute it, but as it does not evaporate rapidly, it is better to use a special degreasing fluid for cleaning an oily engine. Petrol will also dissolve oil and grease, but because of its obvious dangers its use is not advised.

Peroxide dissolved in an equal quantity of water will remove stains caused by most drinks and other liquids. It acts as a bleach and reduces the appearance of mildew.

Dilute oxalic acid may be used to reduce stains in wood. This is a poison and should be carefully used and stored. Domestic bleach can also be used to reduce discoloration in wood.

Warm water with detergent added

may have to follow some of the other solvents to remove them so their effect is not too drastic.

see also PAINT; PAINTING TOOLS; PAINTING AND VARNISHING.

Spars (Fig. 56)

Wooden spars, particularly if softwood, should be well protected with varnish, to minimize wear and prevent the entry of water. Check the security of fastenings and plug holes where screws have loosened.

Where wood or metal spars are grooved for roped edges of sails, check the groove, particularly after varnishing or cleaning. A pull-through can be made by thickening the end of a length of rope with cloth (A) so it fits closely in the groove. If there is hardened glue or varnish that cannot be reached with a narrow chisel or knife, a washer on a shaft (B) can be drawn through. If necessary, file the shaft to pass along

the groove. The pull-through can be used to wax the inside of the groove to help the sail to slide easily. Melt paraffin wax in a can over moderate heat and dip the pull-through in it.

see also FASTENINGS; HALYARDS; MASTS; SCARFING.

Spiling (Fig. 57)

There are many places about a boat where it is impossible to get the shape of a part which has to be fitted by direct measurement. The boatbuilder's method of doing this is called 'spiling'. Measurements may be used, or a shape may be obtained with little reference to a rule.

To get the shape and size of a twisted curved opening, a strip of wood is prepared with a centreline and other lines across it at intervals. This is of no particular width, but is almost as long as the opening. It is cramped or held to the curve in the opening, then measure-

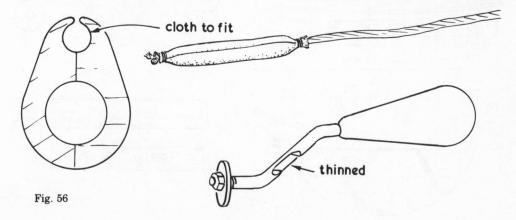

cloth to fit

thinned

Fig. 56

ments are taken at each side of the crossing lines (A). If the wood is then removed and placed on the material that is to make the repair, the measurements can be repeated and a lath sprung through the points to get the correct outline (B).

If the shape of part of the inside of the hull has to be matched for an engine bearer, a piece of plywood can be fixed temporarily above the position, with its lower straight edge parallel with the point the top of the bearer will reach. A spiling stick is made with a point to one side and long enough to overlap the plywood spiling board (C).

The stick is put against the hull in many positions and the other end pencilled around (D). This should be done at any angles of stringers or other parts

and at enough points on curves to allow a lath to be sprung to shape.

The spiling board is removed and put at the correct distance from the edge of the bearer and the spiling stick repositioned in all its marked places, while each point is marked around (E). This gives positions on the outline that will be correct when lines are drawn through them.

Splicing (Fig. 58)

A splice puts a more secure loop or joint into a rope than can be achieved by knotting. For a permanent fastening it is safer and more seamanlike. Although there are a great many splices, the one most commonly needed is an eye splice

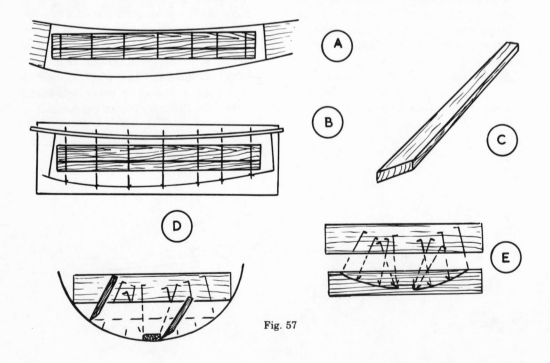

Fig. 57

in three-stranded rope. Such things as long and short splices for joining ropes and a back splice as an alternative to a whipping are rarely needed. A splice between a wire and a fibre rope may be needed on a halyard. New splices have been devised for synthetic braided ropes. Some of these are complicated and depend on the method of rope construction used.

The basic eye splice in three-strand rope is the same whether it is natural or synthetic fibre, except more tucks are advisable for synthetics. To make an eye splice, bend back enough of the rope to make the eye, with more than enough for splicing. It is easier to make a neat job with some excess length to handle than with strands little more than the final length. Open the strands to be tucked. To keep the remainder of the rope in shape it is advisable to put on a temporary whipping for many synthetics (A). Open the rope where the first tuck is to come. This can usually be done by twisting, but it may be necessary to use a spike or fid. Push one of the end strands under a main strand – note that the tucked strand crosses the other. It should be 'against the lay', not with it. Regard this as the front of the splice and arrange the other two end strands as shown (B).

Tuck the end strand nearer the eye, going in where the first tucked end comes out (C). Turn the splice over and find the main strand that still has no end strand under it. Tuck the other end

strand under this, but make sure it also goes against the lay (D).

Pull the end strands through to get an even tension and arrange them all in the same plane around the rope. You should now have an end strand emerging from each space in the rope (E). The temporary whipping may be removed now or later.

From this stage, each end is taken in turn over the next main strand and under the one after that (F). When this has been done with all three, even the tension and see that all are emerging in the same plane around the rope. Do this with each end strand again, so that each one will have gone under a main strand three times. For natural fibre rope this is enough, but for synthetics another round of tucks is advisable.

A splice can be left with the ends cut off at this stage, but for neatness it is better to taper the strands and tuck them again. Use a knife to scrape away the projecting strands to about half thickness. Twist the remaining fibres and tuck them. Cut off fairly close and seal with a flame, but be careful not to melt any part of a main strand. The splice can be made more tidy by rolling between the hands or two boards, not underfoot as this may introduce dirt. A common fault in this and other tucked splices is to tuck at a steep angle so the end strands almost continue along the rope. They should go around the rope at about the same angle as the main strands.

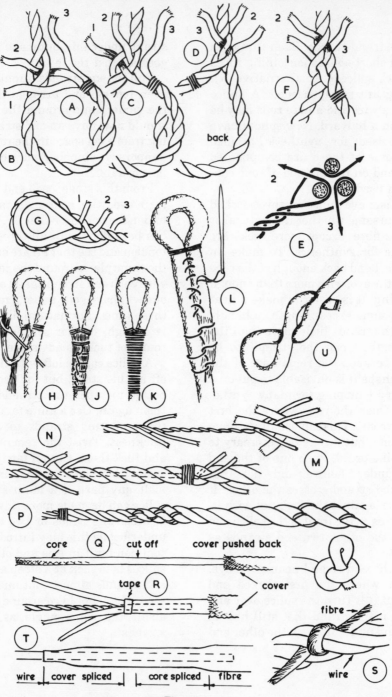

Fig. 58

An eye splice is often needed around a thimble, where it must be tight enough to keep in place under load. With the rope around the thimble tuck the first strand close to the thimble (G). The thimble can be taken out while the other two strands are tucked loosely. It is then replaced and the end strands pulled tight before carrying on with further tucks.

A variation on a Flemish eye can be used for braided rope which consists of a plaited exterior over straight yarns. Unlay and straighten yarns for a distance equal to fifteen to eighteen times the rope diameter. It may be helpful to put temporary whippings at the limit of the eye (H). Pull up to half the straight yarns through the rope close to the eye. How many can be got through depends on how tightly the rope is made. This may be done with a needle, although an awl with a hole, such as a football lacer, can be used.

Lay all the yarns down the rope, keeping their full size for most of their length, but cut some off to cause a taper towards the end. Use sail twine or other light line to seize the yarns with half hitches (J), then serve over tightly with stouter line (K).

A variation of this, which should be stronger, has a length of unlaid rope laid alongside the main part and sewn to it with large stitches, then the tapered straightened strands are seized down (L) and the whole thing served over.

Other splices in braided rope vary according to the rope construction and some need special tools, so refer to makers' instructions.

Where three-strand fibre rope is to be spliced to seven-strand wire rope and the difference in thickness is not much, it is possible to cut out the wire rope heart and pair the remaining strands so the two ropes can be tucked into each other like a short splice, but usually the fibre rope is appreciably thicker and this type of splice is impossible.

One way is to unlay the wire rope and cut out the heart, then take alternate wire strands and lay them up into a three-strand rope. Marry the ends of this with the strands of the fibre rope (M). Put a temporary seizing over this junction. Lay up the fibre rope strands around the wire until they can mate with the other three wire ends (N). Within reason, the further these points are apart, the stronger will be the splice. The junctions are shown close for convenience in illustrating. At each junction wrap each wire strand around the fibre rope strand it is already under. Do this three or four times. Cut off the ends, but allow enough to bury inside the fibre rope. If possible, separate the individual wires and work them into the fibre rope with a needle. Taper the ends of the fibre rope strands, lay them around the wire and put a tight seizing over their ends (P).

How the splice is made with braided rope and seven- or nineteen-strand wire will vary, but the following method can be adapted. The example is seven-strand wire and double-braided fibre ropes. Sizes suit the usual small yacht ropes. Knot the fibre rope about 1 m (3 ft) back from the end and slide the cover back from the end, so about 25 cm (10 in) can be cut off (Q). Tightly seize the end of the wire or seal it with solder. Open up some of the core and push the end of the wire into the part that has not been unlaid. Allow some of the exterior core fibres to lay up into three strands for about 10 cm (4 in). Wax will help keep these in shape. How far the wire goes into the core depends on circumstances, but 15 cm (6 in) is reasonable. Tape or whip the joint temporarily (R).

Tuck the fibre rope end strands into the wire rope, letting each end go under two wire strands, then wrap it around again (S). Go on to another two wire strands and do this again. Cut off the ends. Work the cover back over all this and make sure all slack has been taken up. It may be sufficient to seize down the cover over the wire rope, or the end of the cover can be unlaid to make up into three strands which are tucked into the wire rope in the same way as the core, so the splice has two sets of tucks (T).

For the double sheets of a large head sail there may be two ropes separately spliced to a shackle or ring attached to the sail, but for smaller sails one rope may form both parts of the sheet. The attachment eye may be tightly seized to a thimble or there is a simple lock-tuck splice that can be used on stranded rope or braided rope that is not too tightly laid.

Open one part of the rope with a spike and push the whole of the other part through it, then a short distance away open the rope that was tucked and pass the first part through it (U). This is strong enough with no more treatment, but for neatness it can be served over. A similar idea can be used for a temporary eye in the end of a rope, except the end is tucked twice instead of each part being tucked alternately.

see also KNOTS; RIGGING, RUNNING; ROPE; WHIPPING.

Split pins (cotter pins) (Fig. 59)

Split pins are used to lock nuts and other parts of boat equipment. Common split pins will rust. Brass split pins are not as strong and will deteriorate in a salt atmosphere. Only salt-water-resistant, stainless steel split pins should be used on seagoing craft. It is good practice not to re-use a split pin, as it may break after bending more than once. However, split pins usually survive one re-use.

Usually, the ends of a pin are bent close to the object it fits (A). This keeps the ends out of the way. There is less risk of breakage due to sharp bends if the ends are only spread (B). With a

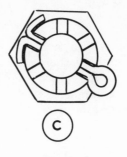

Fig. 59

castellate nut the ends may be spread over the nut (C), but strength is probably greater with the flats of the pin the other way and one leg over the nut and the other along or over the bolt (D).

see also SHEAR PINS.

Steel hulls

Steel should be kept painted, with touching-up as necessary, using the correct primer if starting from bare steel. A rust-inhibiting fluid can be used for minor rusting.

In an emergency a holed steel hull can have the pierced area cleaned of loose paint, then thick paint put on and canvas pressed into it and painted over. Bitumastic paint is suitable.

A hole in a steel hull can be filled with glassfibre and resin or one of the filler compounds sold for repairing car bodies. For a permanent repair the hole should

be cleaned up and glassfibre arranged to overlap inside as well as fill the hole in a similar way to a glassfibre hull. The outside can be cleaned off level and painted over.

Greater damage to a steel hull can be repaired with concrete, which will bond to clean steel. Support a piece of greased plywood outside and arrange wood inside to limit the spread of concrete. If possible arrange the concrete to come between frames or other attachments inside the hull. Arrange strands of wire between these parts holding wire netting, to reinforce the concrete. Use a concrete mixture with the minimum amount of water and lay it with a trowel so as to fill the hole, take in the reinforcing wires and build up to a reasonable thickness inside. Remove the greased plywood outside and use a power sander to bring the concrete flush. If possible, leave for a month before painting, but if necessary the boat may go afloat soon after the concrete has hardened.

see also GLASSFIBRE.

Stern tube (Fig. 60)

If the drive to the propeller is via a shaft through a stern tube or shaft log, there may be a metal outboard bearing, which is lubricated by a screw-down greaser at the inboard end. If a water-lubricated outboard bearing is used, there may still be a greaser feeding only the inboard bearing. There is a gland forward of the greaser and this may need repacking.

There is a special stern gland grease that should be used to top up the greaser. For the gland there is a square-section packing. The gland nut usually has a locking device. With this nut released, a section of packing can be withdrawn and examined as a guide to size. A new piece has to be cut so its ends butt closely. It is not merely wrapped around to overlap. Use the shaft or a piece of wood the same diameter and cut

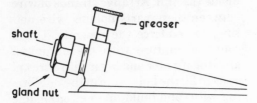

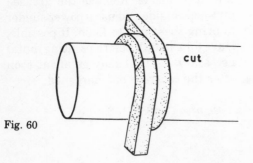

Fig. 60

at an angle through an overlapping length of packing to make a new ring.

Stoppings

Stoppings and fillers are used to fill cracks and holes, or make up unevenness. Caulking is a form of stopping. Stoppings and fillers differ from glues and adhesives in merely filling spaces and not providing any strength in the joint. An exception is the use of glue mixed with sawdust, which can be used as both glue and filler in a joint that would be too wide for plain glue to be effective without losing its strength through crazing.

Paint manufacturers sell stopping material to suit their paints. There is no one stopping that can be used under any type of paint, although an epoxy solvent-less stopper can be covered by most finishes. Most stoppings can be pressed into a hole and left to set, with little fear of contraction. However, it is usual to leave a little excess and sand this level afterwards. Where the surface is rough a filler may be trowelled on. This could be the same material as a stopping, but made more liquid by the appropriate thinner. The effect of the filler on wood is to fill pores and irregularities, so the sanded surface is more even.

Paint stoppings and fillers are often applied after the first coat of paint, depending on the maker's instructions.

Plastic wood is a stopping that sets with more woodlike qualities. It can be applied to wood and may actually build up to a limited extent. For instance, a crack or split that has a small part of the wood actually broken away on a projecting profile, can be made good with plastic wood then cut and sanded to shape before painting over. This might also be done, if more strength is needed, with a glue and sawdust mixture.

No boat is absolutely rigid. Some older planked wooden boats are very obviously flexible, but even a glassfibre boat assembled from only two or three major mouldings, is liable to work. This means that doing something simple like walking on a deck causes joints to flex or move slightly. Consequently, many joints should not be too rigidly made. The usual glues set very rigid and undue strain on them may cause cracking, probably of wood fibres alongside the glue line. It is better to waterproof such joints with a flexible stopping and increase the number of mechanical fastenings to compensate for the lack of glue.

A flexible stopping is also needed where there are open cracks, deck leaks, drips around windows or any of the other leakage problems above the waterline. The usual flexible jointing compound is puttylike and never sets really hard, although some types form a skin that will take paint. The best-known is Seelastik.

Of course, stoppings generally can only be expected to bond and be waterproof if the surfaces to which they are applied are dry. There is a flexible acrylic stopper or sealer that will bond effectively to metal or glass. Many other stoppings are intended mainly for wood. If stopping has to be applied to a damp surface a latex stopping will adhere and can be painted over, but except in emergency, surfaces being stopped should be dry.

Some stoppings and fillers come in tubes and can be squeezed directly into a hole. If the stopping is in a can it can be spread and pressed into place with a putty knife or screwdriver. A stopping only partly filling a can will harden during storage. To prevent this, fill the space above the stopping with a damp cloth to exclude air.

Some stoppings sold for cabinetwork and other purposes ashore will not stand up to conditions afloat. They may not be waterproof to a sufficient degree, although they can be used in a bathroom. Check that anything offered is specified for boats. Some stoppings, such as Brummer, are made in boat as well as other grades.

see also CAULKING; PAINT; PAINT STRIPPING; PAINTING AND VARNISHING; VARNISH.

Terminals

There can be a considerable loss due to poor connections in the low voltage electrical system of a boat and particularly of its engine. Where possible, connections should be avoided by using stout cable from point to point in a circuit, avoiding joints. Soldered joints are preferable to screwed or other mechanical joints. However, there will be many terminals that need periodic attention.

Meeting surfaces should be scraped, rubbed with abrasive paper or wire brushed. Clean the wires and make sure all strands of a multi-strand cable make contact. Cable ends are best provided with an end to fit the terminal. If the wire goes directly on the terminal, twist strands tightly around each other then take the wire around a screwed terminal in the direction of tightening, before screwing down.

Coat the terminals – particularly battery terminals – with the jelly sold for the purpose. If this is unavailable, use petroleum jelly (Vaseline). Electrical work is vulnerable in the damp conditions of a boat and terminals can be a weak link, so clean them and check their tightness frequently.

Thimbles (Fig. 61)

A thimble used in the end of a rope may be made of several metals or plastic. A thimble in a stainless steel rope eye should be stainless steel. Sometimes it is brass. Check this for corrosion. A galvanized steel thimble may suffer from rust where the zinc has worn away, but the thickness is normally sufficient for this not to affect strength. Cleaning will be for the sake of appearance.

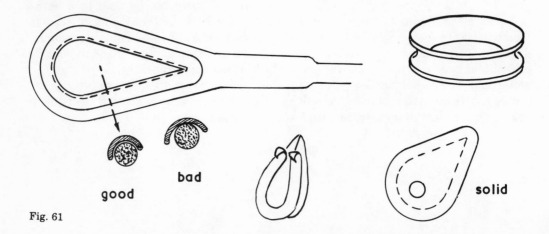

good   bad   solid

Fig. 61

A nylon or other plastic thimble is suitable for fibre rope and bearing against other plastic or wood. If it is attached to a metal fitting, examine it for wear, which can be rapid. The groove in a thimble should match the rope used, otherwise the cross-section of the rope may pull out of shape and be weakened. If the thimble is made from sheet metal, it can be hammered to closely conform to the rope after splicing and before subjecting to load. The points of a sheet metal thimble can be bent back to allow a splice to be made very close, then hammered back again later.

Tingles (Fig. 62)

The simplest repair to a damaged plank of a wooden boat is to put a tingle as a patch on the outside. With the overlap-

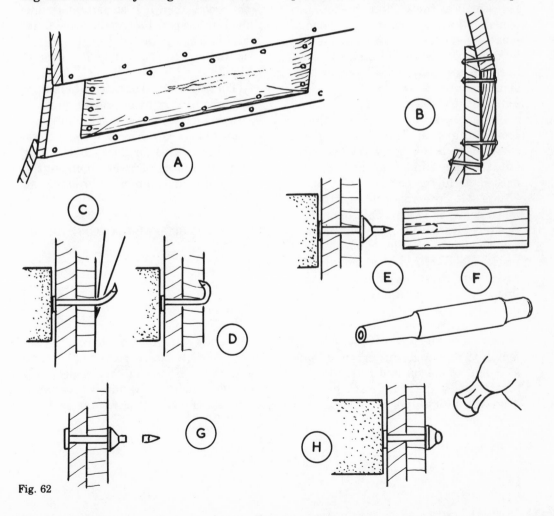

Fig. 62

ping planks of a clinker hull, such a tingle with its edges faired off is acceptable as a permanent repair. With carvel or other flush planking it may be rather ugly and then should only be considered a temporary repair. Traditionally, the tingle was fixed down on paint-soaked canvas, but it is better now to use one of the puttylike jointing compounds that never completely harden.

The tingle should be of similar wood to the hull, if possible, although not necessarily as thick. Plane the top edge to match the plank above, allow enough length to easily cover the damage and let there be enough width to cover, but keep the lower edge above the next line of nails (A), unless the damage goes low. Fair off the three exposed edges (B).

If the planking is thick enough to provide a grip and there is not much curve in the plank, screws can be used, but it is more likely that nails will be needed. Drill for fastenings at about 75 mm (3 in) intervals – closer if there is much curve or twist. For a temporary repair, galvanized iron or copper nails can be driven through and clenched inside. Hold an iron block against the outside and curve the point over a spike first (C), before burying it in the wood (D).

For a permanent nailed repair use copper nails and roves. Choose a nail length that will go through and leave sufficient to cut off and rivet over the rove. Drill a slightly undersize hole and drive the nail through. Hold an iron block or hammer against the head and drive on the rove. A piece of wood with a hole in the end will do for a few fastenings (E). A hollow punch or roving iron is better (F).

Use top or side cutters or cutting pliers to take the end off the nail about 2 mm (1/16 in) above the rove (G). Still with the head supported, use a ball pane or cross pane hammer to spread the end over the rove (H). Do this lightly. Heavy blows may make the nail buckle inside the wood, then if it straightens under load, the repair may leak. After fixing all nails and roves, go over them again so further riveting will pull the tingle tight.

If a tingle has to be fitted where there is considerable twist and it might be impossible to make wood conform, a piece of lead can be used. It could be the sheet type used for household roofing. Round off its corners. Bed it on jointing compound and hammer it to shape as it is fitted.

see also CLINKER PLANKING; FASTENINGS.

Tool kit

Any craft being used offshore is dependent on its own resources in an emergency. Even an inland cruiser may not find help immediately available. Consequently, it is advisable to carry spares and a tool kit with its contents related to the type of boat and the cruising being undertaken. Limitations are mainly due to available space. There are attractions about dual-purpose tools, but some that are offered are of poor quality. Tools taken afloat should be the best for their purpose. Do not be tempted to regard something discarded from the home workshop as being good enough for the boat. It may let you down.

Screwdrivers in several sizes and with points to suit all types of screw head are needed. There are kits with bits to fit one handle that will do for smaller screws, but one or more large screwdrivers will be used for other things, such as levering, besides screwing. Spanners are a problem. For engine parts it is advisable to have fixed spanners to suit. For general purposes one or more adjustable wrenches may do, particularly the type that can be locked on to the nut. This will also serve as a small vice. Have a good pair of pliers that will cut wire. Any hammer of moderate size will do for general purposes. A centre-punch and a few flat-ended punches of different sizes will be useful. If there is nothing else in the tool box that can be used for hammering on, include a small iron block.

A 'junior' hacksaw and some spare blades will do most metal sawing. Half-round files can be used on flats or hollows. A 'second-cut' one about 25 cm (10 in) will do general metal filing, but have a wallet of warding files for intricate work.

Metal drilling will have to be by hand. Have a compact wheel brace with a hollow handle to hold a few bits.

For cutting wood carry a small hand saw of good quality and not too fine teeth. For fine cuts you can use your hacksaw. Instead of a plane, carry a Surform tool with spare flat and curved blades. A 12 mm (½ in) bevel-edged chisel should be a first choice, but have a wider one as well, if there is space. A woodworking brace is bulky. A hole in wood bigger than the size of the metal-working drill can usually be 'worried out' with a chisel after drilling with the wheel brace.

If you are sailing for any great length of time, have thread or sail twine, a few needles of different sizes and a palm.

You will probably be carrying a knife and spike. These are important, but it is important that the knife and any other edge tools are sharp. You can carry a small oilstone. If it is bought specially, get a two-sided one, with coarse and fine surfaces. A useful alternative is a flat scythe stone. This is lubricated with water instead of oil. Tools can be rubbed on it, or it can be used in one hand like a file.

Much measuring on board can be by direct comparison, but include an expanding rule so you can note sizes of parts to be made at home. Keep a pencil in the tool box. Chalk is also sometimes needed for marking out.

Have a stock of screws, nails and all the bits and pieces that go with a boat. In an emergency ordinary iron screws might be used, but having the right screws available avoids the need for changing screws later. Include some self-adhesive waterproof tape, which makes a good repair bandage for many things. Ordinary boatbuilding glue is not quick enough in action for an emergency, but a pair of tubes of quick-acting epoxy glue will allow repairs to wood and other materials to be effected in fifteen minutes or so.

Most tools have to be steel, so they are liable to rust. Greasing them may be advisable if they are left for some time, but this is messy and wiping before use is a nuisance. It is better to pack silica gel in the form of crystals or impreg-nated paper with the tools, so it absorbs moisture. If the material becomes satu-rated, it can be dried and used again.

A plastic box, of the type intended for angler's equipment, does not attract moisture like wood and does not corrode like steel. It is also easier on the edges of cutting tools. An alternative is a stout canvas bag, thoroughly treated with waterproofing solution. If this has a side opening which laces and a pair of carry-ing handles, it can be put down almost anywhere without risk of it causing damage and it may be hoisted aloft by its handles for a repair above decks. If saws, chisels and other cutting tools cannot be fitted into compartments that protect them, make wood or plastic sheaths to cover the cutting edges.

see also DESICCATOR.

Varnish

Marine varnish may be regarded as clear paint. A conventional varnish is applied like paint and there are no separate primer and undercoats – the same varnish is used throughout, although the first coat may be thinned to achieve a deeper penetration.

A twin-pack varnish may be polyurethane based and some makers use the term 'lacquer', which should not be confused with that name used for other finishes ashore. A twin-pack finish is only suitable for use over itself and should not be applied over conventional varnish. However, conventional varnish may follow the twin-pack type.

Other clear finishes, such as sprayed cellulose lacquer and shellac, are unsuitable for use afloat. Cabin furniture and other internal things that would have these finishes or polish ashore are better finished with marine varnish.

see also PAINT; PAINT STRIPPING; PAINTING TOOLS; PAINTING AND VARNISHING; STOPPINGS.

Ventilation

Parts of a cabin boat can become sealed compartments in which air will stagnate, condensation will take place, gas and fumes accumulate and conditions develop which would not be tolerated at home. There are occasions in bad weather or sea conditions, when it is necessary to seal the boat, but in normal circumstances there should be a change of air taking place.

To ventilate any compartment it is necessary to let air out as well as in, and the entrance and exit are better for being at the extremes of the volume of air. In a small cabin boat there can be plenty of ventilation due to the opening of doors, hatches and windows. The circulation of air when a boat is under way may be from aft forward within the cabin, so any ventilators should be arranged to allow for this.

Apart from general ventilation a circulation of air within small compartments is important, to minimize the risk of rot. Holes drilled are more effective than small plastic ventilators, particularly if at opposite ends of a compartment. When a boat is left, it is helpful to prop up bunk tops, open lockers or leave doors ajar. The needs of security have to be balanced against the needs of ventilation.

Covering with plastic sheeting wrapped closely may trap moisture. The impermeable material will not allow moist air to escape. Such covers should be held away from the surface so air can circulate.

see also BOTTLED GAS; CONDENSATION; FIREFIGHTING EQUIPMENT; HEATERS; PLYWOOD REPAIRS; PRESERVATIVES; ROT; VENTILATORS.

Ventilators (Fig. 63)

It is unlikely that much will need to be done to keep ventilators in order, but leaks are a nuisance. If there is drip from around a ventilator, the only satisfactory treatment is to remove fastenings and bed down the flange in a fresh layer of jointing compound. If there are many fastenings, tighten progressively, working on opposite pairs, so as to squeeze the stopping level and force out air pockets.

Screw-down ventilators may benefit from a coating of graphite grease on the screw. Apply sparingly and work up and down a few times to spread lubricant, then wipe off any surplus which might drip inside.

Dorade-type ventilators, or others with a water trap, should be checked for debris and dirt, so water entering will flow clear and not settle where it may become stagnant.

Cabin bulkhead and under-bunk ventilators, made of metal or plastic, often have very fine holes, which attract dust and cobwebs. If air in a confined space is obviously stagnant or there are signs of accumulated damp, a pattern of small holes drilled in the wood may be better than fixed ventilators. Whatever type of ventilator is used, air should be able to enter in one place and emerge at the other extreme, so one ventilator is never much use. For a confined space there should be two, but a frequently-used door or hatch may provide the second ventilation point.

see also VENTILATION

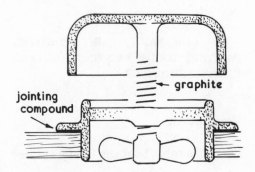

Fig. 63

Water system

The important thing in the servicing of a drinking-water system is the maintenance of purity and cleanliness as well as avoidance of leaks. Although drinking water can be kept safe to use for very long periods, it is advisable to drain and refill when there is an opportunity, so that any solid matter may be washed out. Some water supplies contain minute particles of sand which can damage pump washers and other parts, so if a doubtful source has had to be used for filling, a drain and flush through with water known to be clean is advisable.

If light-coloured or transparent plastic tanks, cans and tubes are used for drinking water, algae may form inside. This will only form in the presence of light, so although a light colour looks more hygienic than a dark one, dark plastic is preferable as it will remain free from algae. Algae can be removed with one of the fluids intended for cleaning dentures. It may work if diluted or it may have to be used full strength, but it should be allowed to stand at the affected part for some time, then be flushed away with clean water.

If the water system is built in and the boat has to be left during a period of frost, the same precautions will have to be taken as with home plumbing. Ideally, the system should be drained, but it may be difficult to remove all water from pipes which may be lower than the drain point or from equipment such as pumps which may allow pockets of water to settle. It may be necessary to break connections and drain individual items. Lagging with cloth or other material may be applied temporarily during a winter lay-up, but it is better to completely drain.

If the system uses plastic pipes there is less risk of damage if water is trapped in them and expands as it freezes, as there is some elasticity which is not present in metal pipes. However, the usual plastic becomes hard and brittle at low temperatures, so it is unwise to rely on flexibility protecting the system. Even if the pipes do not break, joints may be affected. If any part of a water system has frozen check that joints have not moved or loosened.

Most pumps used in water systems have synthetic rubber parts. This material may be used for diaphragms and valves. Wear occurs progressively and inefficiency may not be apparent for some time. A common trouble is for a non-return valve to leak back slightly, so the pump does not deliver water as quickly although it still functions at a lower rate. Hand pumps that function as taps are easily dismantled. Foot and electric pumps may be more complicated, but the makers of the popular types provide kits of replacement parts with instructions, based on the expected wear. If one of these pumps fails it is advisable to get a kit before dismantling, so the correct sequence can be followed.

If a metal water tank of a permanent installation has an inspection panel, it may not be necessary to open this very often, but if the water acquires a taste or smell, it is likely that there is a sediment which should be removed and the tank purified. Sediment may be removed by scraping. A domestic cleaner may have to be used, but all trace of this will have to be washed away. Marine paint manufacturers can supply special paints for the insides of metal water tanks. A glassfibre or plastic tank should not be painted inside.

As a filler only leaks when it is used, examine it when water is passing through. Pipe clips can usually be tightened a little. If there is a persistent leak, moving the pipe clip a short distance along the pipe may cure it, otherwise take the joint apart and smear jointing compound on the metal tube before reclamping the flexible pipe to it.

As water is drawn from a tank air must be able to enter. See that vent pipes are clear. The action of drawing in air may also pull in fluff and other light materials.

There are not many installations where the waste water goes to a holding tank, to be pumped out later with sewage. It is more usual for water from wash basins and showers to go out through the hull. Any hole in the hull should be regarded as vulnerable, even if it is well above the normal waterline. The skin fitting should be properly bedded down in waterproof compound and bolted through a reinforcing block on the inside of the hull. A simple screwed fitting should only be regarded as satisfactory if small and high in the side of an inland cruiser.

The majority of waste water skin fittings do not have a valve for closing them in emergency. This may not matter if the outlet is fairly high, but the waste pipe should be of a stout gauge tube. If metal, it should be secured at both ends with a strong pipe clip. The bore of the waste pipe is usually small when compared with domestic plumbing, but similar debris is usually tipped down a sink outlet with waste water. At lay-up time the pipe should be removed and cleaned out, by poking and the use of hot detergent. If it is left until fitting-out it may be producing a foul smell.

Wheel steering (Fig. 64)

If cable steering is used, both parts may come to one side (A), although in a runabout they may pass both sides (B).

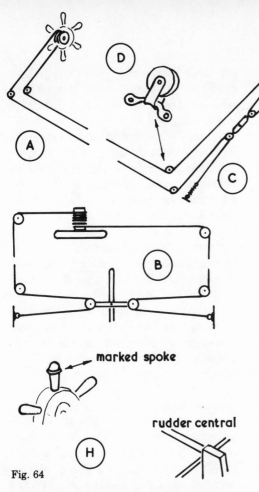

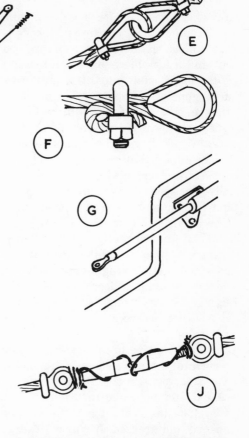

marked spoke

rudder central

Fig. 64

Control may be at a tiller to a rudder or to a connection on an outboard motor. Because this point is not far from the pivot point, leverage is often reduced 2:1 by taking the cables around sheaves and back to the sides (C), to avoid too harsh a movement. Follow through the run of cable to familiarize yourself with the system before inspection or servicing.

Check the cable for wear. Galvanized steel cable may have rusted and some wires broken. Stainless steel cable is less likely to show wire breakages unless the sheaves are very small. For the usual sizes of cable sheaves should be at least 5 cm (2 in) diameter and preferably free to take up a normal position in relation to the pull of the cable (D). Fixed blocks and sheaves out of line are liable to cause wear on the sides of the sheave grooves or on the wire. Wear anywhere on the wire usually means replacement cable is required throughout, unless the damaged cable can be cut and a new piece joined in, usually with loops and clips (E); but this arrangement cannot go around a sheave, so a new cable is more likely. Check the security of wire ends. There are several types of clip. Extra security can be obtained by turning an end back (F). At the steering wheel the cable usually goes several times around a drum, but its centre is secured in some way. Check this screw or other fitting.

When the wheel is put hard over there can be considerable load on the cable and on the fixings of the sheaves it passes around. Check all of these fixings – bolts through are more secure than wood screws and lock nuts are advisable.

An alternative to cable steering is a push–pull cable in a casing. The unit at the steering wheel will probably be sealed and not require attention. At very long intervals it may have to be opened and greased. A run with large curves and minimum attachment points is necessary if internal friction is to be kept to a minimum and the steering action be easy. At the stern end there is a rod action to the tiller or motor. The success of its action depends on the secure mounting of the casing end, which has to resist the reaction to any movement of the rod (G). See that the bracket is firmly bolted on and there is no play when the wheel is operated to the limit both ways. There has to be a slight universal movement. Check that nothing restricts this and lubricate with grease.

Whatever system of remote steering is used, it should be possible to steer with a tiller in an emergency. An outboard motor should retain its tiller and it should be possible to cast off the remote steering without the use of tools. If steering is by a rudder and the tiller is not normally kept mounted, it should be in a rack nearby ready to be fitted and it should be possible to release the remote controls.

A push–pull system is unlikely to need adjustment, but a flexible cable system may suffer from stretch. Springs are often included in the system. These take care of varying tension when a tiller swings, as well as allowing for some stretch. If stretch has to be taken up, this can be done at the ends of the cable by drawing wire through a clip to a new position, but this should be done equally each side to keep the correct relation between the wheel and the helm. With a spoked wheel the marked spoke should be upright when the rudder is central (H). With a car-type wheel its pattern of spokes should be level. For finer adjustment, rigging screws can be included in each part of the cable system and locked when the correct tension has been obtained, using wire if no other method of locking is provided (J).

If remote steering is to an outboard motor mounted in a cutout transom, check that there is sufficient movement both ways – 45 degrees is usually enough. Make sure this is still obtainable if the motor tilts after hitting an obstruction. As there will probably be cables controlling throttle and gear change as well, see that none of these foul each other or the steering arrangements in any position.

see also RUDDER.

Whipping (Fig. 65)

A loose end of rope will soon unlay to open yarns and fibres in a 'mare's tail' that cannot be laid up again, so the rope has to be cut and a part wasted. Synthetic ropes may be sealed with heat. Use a cigarette lighter or a match until the end is beginning to become liquid, then roll it between moistened finger and thumb. This cannot be done with natural fibre ropes and they must be whipped. A whipping, as well as sealing, is advisable for synthetic rope. Checking the state of ropes' ends should be ongoing maintenance throughout the season as a rope that loses its whipping cannot be left if waste is to be avoided.

Whipping means binding the end of a rope so the strands and yarns cannot unlay. Although done mainly to preserve the rope, it also reduces and stiffens the end so it is easier to knot or pass through a hole. There are a very large number of whippings, but only two or three are needed for modern yacht ropework.

Whipping line is strong thread and should not be too thick in relation to the size of rope. Thick line on thin rope may soon come adrift. Whipping line is sold in hanks or on reels, but for smaller ropes, stout sewing thread is suitable. Use line that matches the rope – do not use natural fibre line on synthetic rope. It is helpful to draw the line through a piece of beeswax or a candle before use. This causes the line to stay put and a neater whipping results. It also waterproofs natural fibre line.

The West Country whipping is simple and suitable for all kinds of rope, as well as shock cord, insulation and anything else that has to be squeezed tight. Most whippings are satisfactory if made about as long as the diameter of the rope, so start rather more than this distance from the end and put the centre of a short length of line behind the rope. Bring the ends to the front and knot them (A). Take them to the back and knot them again. Continue knotting back and front, close to the previous knots, until a sufficient length has been covered, then make the last knot into a reef knot and cut off the ends (B).

A better whipping has the line through the rope as well as around it. This sailmaker's whipping is made on three-strand rope by opening a short distance and laying in a loop of whipping line so it encircles one strand and

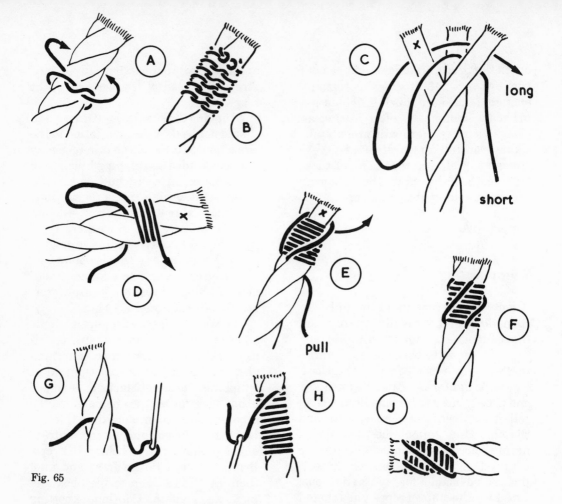

Fig. 65

the ends come out of the opposite space. One end can be quite short, but the other is long enough to put on the whipping turns (C). Lay the rope strands together again. Hold the short end and the loop down the rope, while turns are put tightly around the rope with the long end (D).

When sufficient turns are on, hold them tight while the loop is lifted over the outside of the whipping and over the strand it is already encircling. Pull the short end and this will make the two sides of the loop follow up as snaking turns over two gaps between strands (E).

The short end is left projecting from the only space where there is no snaking turn. Take it up over the outside of the whipping following this space and

190

into the centre of the end of the rope (F), where it is tied with a reef knot to the long end.

That whipping may only be used when the strands of rope can be opened. If they are already sealed or the rope is braided or of other construction, a similar result is achieved with a palm and needle whipping. A needle is put on the thread and passed through the rope (G). The short end is laid up the rope and the rest of the line used to whip tightly over it, then the needle passed through the rope again (H).

With stranded rope, let the needle come out at a space, then put on the outside snaking turns following the spaces between rope strands, letting the needle go in one space and out another, until all three spaces have snaking strands (J). Finish by passing the needle down through the whipping.

This can be done on braided line or rope of other form, but the snaking strands may be arranged in line with the rope and it is simplest to arrange four of them.

see also RIGGING, RUNNING; SPLICING.

Winches

Halyard and sheet winches need little attention, except for lubrication, and some types can only be satisfactorily dealt with by partial dismantling to introduce grease or oil to the right parts. Lack of lubrication increases friction and reduces the purchase obtained for a given effort. Pawls should be seen to drop into place properly all round.

A winch used for the anchor cable needs similar attention. Security of wheels and axles should be checked. Keys should be fully into their keyways and any Allen screws or other screwed fastenings should be tight. The system for preventing the winch running back may need a pawl filing or its position altered. If there is a friction brake or clutch, check it for wear and correct adjustment. Check the secure attachment of the winch to the deck. Examine underneath for pulled fastenings and use pads or larger washers if necessary.

If a winch uses an oil bath, check the oil level and renew the oil if it has been in use some time. Check the effectiveness of any oil seals, and replace where necessary. Some small winches have plastic bearings. These should not be oiled.

Window moulding (Fig. 66)

Cabin windows in many small cruisers, whether glass or plastic, are set in a moulding, which is forced tight between the window and the plywood or glassfibre side of the cabin by an inserted filler strip (A). Usually the joint in the main moulding is at the bottom and the joint in the filler strip at the top.

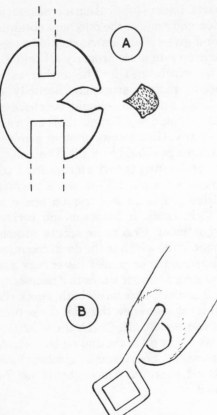

Fig. 66

A reasonably precise fit is needed if this type of window moulding is to be successful. If a broken window has to be replaced, use the old window as a pattern if possible. Otherwise, or with a new window, make a stiff card or hardboard pattern and try this in place. The shape is the outline of the window open-

ing less the thickness at the core of the moulding and just a little more for fitting. Round off the edge of a Perspex window for ease in fitting.

Position the moulding around the opening. Use a fine brush to put soapy water around the groove. Work the window into the moulding groove. A screwdriver may be needed to bend the lip of the moulding back for the last springing in. Most moulding is soft enough to allow this, but in very cold weather it is helpful to soften the moulding for a few minutes in hot water, just before fitting it. Leave it wet as this helps provide lubrication when fitting the window.

With the window in the groove the filler strip has to be forced in. There is a special tool for this (B), which may be hired. The strip goes through the tool and projects through the shaped end. The first short length of filler is forced into the moulding, possibly with the aid of a screwdriver, then the tool pressed into the moulding so the working end goes below the edges of the groove. It is drawn along so the filler strip passes into the groove. Soapy water dabbed ahead of the tool aids its movement. Without the special tool it is possible to insert the filler strip a little at a time by lifting the edges of the groove with a screwdriver and pressing the filler down. This is tedious, but may be acceptable for work on a single window.